P9-DHR-462

CULTURE SMART!
USA

Gina Teague

Graphic Arts Center Publishing®

Tulare County Library

First published in Great Britain 2004
by Kuperard, an imprint of Bravo Ltd.

Copyright © 2004 Kuperard

All rights reserved. No part of this publication may be reprinted
or reproduced, stored in a retrieval system, or transmitted in any
form or by any means without prior permission in writing from
the Publishers.

Series Editor Geoffrey Chesler
Design DW Design

Simultaneously published in the U.S.A. and Canada
by Graphic Arts Center Publishing Company
P. O. Box 10306, Portland, OR 97296-0306

Library of Congress Cataloging-in-Publication Data

Teague, Gina.
USA: a quick guide to customs and etiquette / Gina Teague.
    p. cm. – (Culture smart!)
Includes bibliographical references and index.
ISBN 1-55868-790-4 (softbound)
1. United States–Social life and customs. 2. National characteristics,
American. 3. United States–Description and travel. 4. Etiquette–United
States. I. Title. II. Series.
E161.T43 2004
973–dc22

                                    2004005824

Printed in Hong Kong

Cover image: Guggenheim Museum, New York.
Travel Ink/Andrew Cowin

The image on page 18 is reproduced with
the permission of Carolyn Eardley.

CultureShock!Consulting and Culture Smart! guides both contribute
to and regularly feature in the weekly travel program "Fast Track" on
BBC World TV.

About the Author

GINA TEAGUE is a trainer and writer on cross-cultural management, international relocation, and global career development. A native of the United Kingdom, she has lived and worked in France, Spain, Brazil, the U.S.A., and Australia. During her sixteen years in America, she developed a successful intercultural consultancy serving the corporate, academic, and non-profit sectors. She also gained an M.A. in Organizational Psychology and an EdM in Counseling Psychology from Columbia University, and produced two "native New Yorker" children. Gina has written extensively on expatriate adjustment and career management issues for industry journals and Web sites. A principal and cofounder of Isis Group International, an intercultural training company, she has recently relocated to Sydney, Australia.

Other Books in the Series

Other titles are in preparation. For more information, contact: info@kuperard.co.uk

The publishers would like to thank **CultureShock!Consulting** for its help in researching and developing the concept for this series.

CultureShock!Consulting

We are all likely at some time to be dealing with other cultures—foreign visitors at home, e-mails from abroad, overseas sales agents, multicultural teams within our organization, or a new foreign management structure.

CultureShock!Consulting creates tailor-made seminars and consultancy programs to meet all types of corporate, public sector, and individual intercultural needs. It provides pre- and post-assignment programs, as well as ongoing "in-the-field" counseling worldwide.

For details, see www.cultureshockconsulting.com

contents

contents

Map of the USA

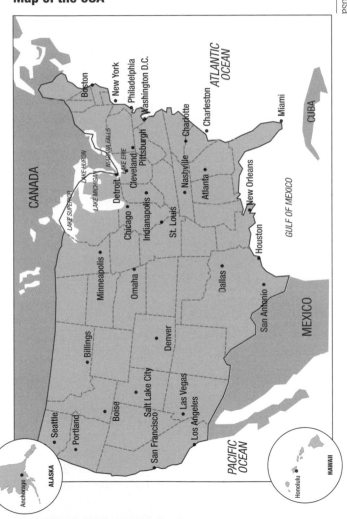

introduction

introduction

In today's global village, who can afford not to understand the U.S.A, the only remaining superpower and, by most standards, the world's most important nation? Many facets of American life have been eagerly embraced around the world. Yet the sense of "just like in the movies" familiarity that first-time visitors often feel can be misleading. Underneath the gleaming smile of popular culture lies a rich and complex society, brimming with contrasts and contradictions. Ostentatious wealth coexists with real poverty, bucolic towns with cities that scrape the sky. It is a culture of go-getters, of high tech, high achievers who have put a man on the moon and count Mars as their latest scientific sandbox. It is also a deeply spiritual, compassionate country with a quiet devotion to church and charitable works.

The sheer size and diversity of America can be overwhelming. How does one begin to understand a country that spans six time zones?

Culture Smart! USA aims to provide you with a cultural "road map" to explain the *human* dimension of American society. We take you on a tour of the core influences and unique ideals that have shaped American society. These deeply held values drive the behavior and attitudes you will encounter on Main Street and in the workplace. We take the pulse of America today. Ever a work in progress, America bears the challenge of upholding its constitutional principles at home, and the responsibility of being the world's only superpower overseas. On a lighter note, we look at the Americans at work, at home, and at play.

A nation of immigrants, America has an openness and generosity of spirit to newcomers. Visitors will find a dynamic, adventurous, warm people who will accept you on your own terms. There are few cultural *faux pas* that can get you into trouble in this relaxed and informal society. But don't be lulled into a false sense of security, either. Americans hold a firm conviction that theirs is the best country in the world. You'll endear yourself to your hosts by being mindful of this deep pride, and of their cherished ideals.

Finally, a disclaimer. In attempting to portray a nation of 290 million people, one can use only a very broad brush. Generalizations, with all their limitations, are unavoidable. The rule of thumb is: be informed about cultural norms, but be flexible in applying this knowledge. In other words, check your assumptions before entering into any cross-cultural encounter!

culture smart! usa

Key Facts

Official Name	United States of America	
Capital City	Washington, D.C.	
Major Cities by Population	New York, Los Angeles, Chicago, Houston, Philadelphia	
Area	3,675,031 sq. miles (9,518,330 sq. km) which includes the 48 contiguous states and the capital district, and the states of Hawaii and Alaska.	Also includes various territories and dependencies, including American Samoa, Northern Mariana Islands, Palau, Guam, Puerto Rico, and the U.S. Virgin Islands.
Climate	Continental, with extremes of temperature and precipitation.	
Currency	Dollar	
Population	290 million	
Ethnic Makeup	White or mixed race 68.5%; African-American 13%; Hispanic 13% ; Asian 4%; Native American and Alaskan Inuit 1.5%	
Language	English	Many government and commercial services are also provided in Spanish and Chinese.

Religion	Protestant (including Southern Baptist, Methodist, and Episcopalian) 56%; Roman Catholic 27%; Jewish 2%; Muslim 2%; Other 13%.	
Government	Federal Government of 50 states and the District of Columbia. The seat of Government is Washington, D.C. The executive is headed by the President. The bicameral legislative body (Congress) is composed of the Senate and the House of Representatives.	
Media	The main network television channels are ABC, CBS, NBC. The total number of local, cable, and satellite channels exceeds 1,600.	There are 10,000 plus FM and AM radio stations, and over 1,500 daily newspapers.
Electricity	110 volts (60-Hertz)	
Telephone	Country code: 1	To dial out: 011
TV/Video	NTSC system. Pal will only work on multisystem TVs and videos.	
Time Zones	There are four time zones across the American continent. Alaska and Hawaii cover two more. Eastern: GMT minus 5 hrs Central: GMT minus 6 hrs Mountain: GMT minus 7hrs Pacific: GMT minus 8 hrs Alaska: GMT minus 9 hrs Hawaii: GMT minus 10 hrs	

LAND & PEOPLE

Stretching from "sea to shining sea," the United States of America is bordered by Canada to the north and Mexico to the south. People generally think of it as the lower forty-eight states and the District of Columbia (Washington, D.C.) situated in the central portion of the North American continent. With a landmass of 3,675,031 square miles, America is the third-largest country in the world. It has a coast-to-coast span of some 2,700 miles, and is as geographically diverse as it is vast. In addition to "purple mountain majesties and amber fields of grain," the landscape features swampy wetlands, lush rain forests, shimmering deserts, and glacial lakes.

The other two stars on the Stars and Stripes flag represent the states of Alaska (northwest of Canada) and Hawaii (situated in the Central Pacific, 2,500 miles to the west of California). Other territories and dependencies include American Samoa, the Northern Mariana Islands, Palau, and Guam in the Pacific, and Puerto Rico and the U.S. Virgin Islands in the Caribbean Sea.

OLD MAN RIVER

The names of America's waterways indicate the central role they have played in America's history and folklore. Among the major rivers of the east, Boston's Charles and Virginia's James Rivers were named for British monarchs, while the Delaware was named for an English patron, Lord De La Warr. The Hudson River was named for the navigator who followed its meandering course into the uncharted interior of upstate New York. As with many place-names in the U.S.A., the Susquehanna, Potomac, and Roanoke Rivers are derived from Native American words.

The five Great Lakes that create vast inland seas on the border between the U.S.A. and Canada form the largest body of freshwater in the world. The Missouri-Mississippi River system is the longest in North America. Immortalized in the nineteenth-century writings of Mark Twain, the Mississippi was at one time the country's lifeline, connecting the upper Plains states and the South.

CLIMATE

The range of latitudes together with the sheer size
of the landmass produces great variations of
temperature and precipitation. Ranging from
subarctic at its highest elevations to tropical in its
southernmost points, temperatures can range
from below zero in the Great Lakes region to a
balmy 80 degrees in Florida—on the same day!

The continental climate of the central portion
of the country produces extreme conditions
throughout the year. Temperatures in the Great
Plains state of North Dakota have ranged between
a summer high record of 121°F (49°C) and a
winter low of -60°F (-51°C). With no high
elevations to protect it, the interior lowlands are
at the mercy of both the warm southern Gulf
Stream and blasts of arctic air from the north. The
occasional colliding of these incompatible
weather systems produces violent conditions.
Displays of nature at her most ferocious can be
witnessed in the form of blizzards, hailstorms,
tornadoes, and dust storms.

The western mountain states enjoy mild
summers, but the higher elevations are blanketed in
snow throughout the winter months. The low,
desert areas of Arizona and New Mexico experience
hot, dry air, but winters can be surprisingly cold.

The more temperate zones are confined to the
coastal areas, blocked from extending their

moderate influence inland by the Appalachians in the east and the Pacific Coast ranges in the west. The Gulf Stream, a warm ocean current that originates in the Gulf of Mexico and flows northeast across the Atlantic, produces hot, wet, energy-sapping conditions for Florida and the other Gulf Coast states.

Temperatures are moderate year-round on the Pacific Coast, although they start to dip as you venture northward into America's wettest region. The Cascade Range acts as a climatic divide, with the lush western side receiving up to twenty times more precipitation than the dusty plains to the mountains' east.

REGIONS

America's malls and main streets may be taking on a uniform blandness, but there are still rich, diverse cultures to be found at the regional level. People express their regional identity in many ways, not least through the state motto on their license plates. The boundary lines defining each region are often subject to dispute. What follows are definitions from the U.S. government Web site—as official as it gets!

New England
(Maine, New Hampshire, Vermont,
Massachusetts, Connecticut, and Rhode Island.)

> **"Live free or die!"**
> *State motto of New Hampshire*

For such a small region, New England has played
a disproportionate role in the country's political
and cultural development. The town meetings
held by church congregations to voice
opinions and effect change on local
issues, for example, provided the model
for democratic popular government in
America. The religious principles,
political activism, and
industriousness that shaped its
history translate today into a
culture characterized by
conservatism, community involvement, and a
strong work ethic.

Many of the first European settlers were English
Protestants, seeking religious freedom. The area
was also a magnet for anticolonialist sentiment,
providing the setting for the Boston Tea Party and
many of the battles of the ensuing Revolutionary
War. Family fortunes amassed in Boston through
fishing and shipbuilding financed the industrial
revolution in the nineteenth century. The region's

wealth established it as the intellectual and cultural center of the fledgling country.

Today, New England's whaling and manufacturing have been replaced by high-tech industries. However, its history is still evident through the Bostonian accent and the colonial-style houses and white-spired churches. The region is favored by tourists for its rugged coastline and Cape Cod's sandy beaches. Vermont's Green Mountains are home to moose and black bear.

The Middle Atlantic
(New York, New Jersey, Pennsylvania, Delaware, and Maryland.)

> **"Liberty and prosperity"**
> *State motto of New Jersey*

The Mid-Atlantic region has taken center stage for much of the nation's historical and economic activity. Home to New York's Ellis Island, the port of entry for immigrants, the region was the original melting pot into which ambitious newcomers eagerly dived. Today, there are still eight times as many people per square mile in the Northeast than there are in the West. New England's money may have financed the industrial revolution, but it was New Jersey and

Pennsylvania's manpower that stoked the chimneys. New York has not only replaced Boston as the financial capital, but its energy, pace, and intensity fuels—and defines—American capitalism. Historic Philadelphia provided the backdrop for the Declaration of Independence (1776), and the drafting of the U.S. Constitution.

The original farmers and traders of the region were blessed with rich farmlands, vital waterways, and forests teeming with wildlife, timber, and mineral resources. Man has encroached and altered this part of the American landscape more than any other, yet it retains a stunning array of scenic landscapes. The indented coastline features rolling sand dunes and bustling harbor resorts. The lowlands of the Atlantic coastal plain incorporate both the eastern corridor of major metropolises and gently undulating farmlands.

Further inland, the plains bump up against New York's Catskills and Pennsylvania's Allegheny Mountains. These subsidiary ranges are part of the Appalachian Mountain range, which forms an almost unbroken spine running parallel to the East Coast from northern Maine south to Georgia.

The region's waterways are no less impressive. While it may be surrounded by motels and commercial kitsch, the sheer power of Niagara Falls, one of the world's seven natural wonders, is still breathtaking.

The Midwest
(Ohio, Michigan, Indiana, Wisconsin, Illinois, Minnesota, Iowa, parts of Missouri, North Dakota, South Dakota, Nebraska, Kansas, and Eastern Colorado.)

> **"The crossroads of America"**
> *State motto of Indiana*

An agricultural powerhouse of patchwork farms giving way to rolling wheat fields, the northeast corner of America's vast interior plain has long been regarded as the breadbasket of the United States. The rich soil and the landscapes, in many places reminiscent of scenes from the old country, first attracted European immigrants to farm the interior plains of America. Illinois, home to the third-largest city, Chicago, attracted Poles, Germans, and Irish. Scandinavians favored Minnesota, with its familiar forests of birch and pine. Milwaukee is renowned for its European-style taverns and beer festivals.

As western settlement pushed past the

Mississippi, the Midwest was transformed from an outpost into the trading and transportation hub of the developing country. This interior region is also dubbed the "heartland"—a reference to the wholesome values and unpretentious nature of its people, deemed to be representative of the nation in general.

Will it Play in Peoria?

This famous question originated during the vaudeville era. If a newly launched show met the approval of the Peoria (Illinois) audience, the belief was that it would be well received anywhere in the country. To this day, when marketing or political pollsters want to take the pulse of the nation, they still use the Midwest as their testing ground.

Further west, the Dakotas area is rich in both human and paleontological history, featuring Oligocene fossil beds dating back 35 million years. However, the desolate landscape evokes images of the more recent past, when the Black Hills and Badlands region formed the backdrop for battles between U.S. soldiers, land-hungry settlers, and Native American tribes. The constant battle against extreme weather and dust-bowl conditions has forged a stoic and taciturn nature. Meeting the open horizons on its western edges, the flat prairie land of the Great Plains rises majestically to form the Rockies.

The West
(Colorado, Wyoming, Montana, Utah, California, Nevada, Idaho, Oregon, Washington.)

> "Eureka" ("I have found it")
> *State motto of California*

The Rocky Mountains dissect the western portion of the continent, stretching from Montana in the north to New Mexico in the south. Moving west, the glacial basins and plains of the Intermontane Plateau include Utah's Salt Lake City, Arizona's Grand Canyon, and California's forbidding Mojave Desert. Closer to the Pacific coast, the Sierra Nevada range runs up through California. Continuing the line through the Pacific Northwest states of Oregon and Washington, the volcanic peaks of the Cascade Mountains extend to the Canadian border.

America's western states have produced legends of grand proportions. The forces of nature seem to have conspired to ward off visitors. Here, the mountain peaks are higher, the deserts deadlier, and the foaming river rapids swifter than anywhere else. Even the wildlife is not for the fainthearted—grizzly bears, mountain lions, and rattlesnakes call this region home. Further natural

barriers have been thrown up relatively recently. In 1906, Point Reyes was at the epicenter of what became known as the San Francisco earthquake, with the infamous San Andreas Fault creating a peninsula that juts ten miles into the Pacific. In 1980, the violent eruption of Mount St. Helens ejected ash sixteen miles up into the sky.

California is equally popular for the attractions of its cities, Los Angeles and San Francisco for example, and its stunning natural beauty. Fun-loving, energetic Californians brag they have world-class ski slopes, lush vineyards, and endless beaches all in their backyard. The state has the nation's most important and diversified agricultural economy.

Whether the West, the "last frontier," was penetrated and settled because of the people's adventurous, single-minded character, or the tough environment shaped those very traits, is debatable. These days, newcomers are attracted here for its sense of space, easygoing nature, and tolerance of alternative lifestyles. What is not in doubt is that the natural wonders of this region provide a playground without parallel for outdoor enthusiasts.

The Southwest
(Western Texas, parts of Oklahoma, New Mexico, Arizona, Nevada, and the southern interior part of California.)

> "Crescit eundo" ("It grows as it goes")
> *State motto of New Mexico*

The desert scapes of the Southwest have a deeply spiritual quality. Arizona's largest city, Phoenix, was so named in 1867 by Darrell Duppa because he thought the desert oasis had sprung from the ashes of an ancient civilization. Actually, Duppa's fertile "oasis" was due to a primitive but effective irrigation project, established centuries before the Europeans' arrival. Other vestiges of ancient civilizations remain in the form of the ninth-century ruins of the scientifically advanced Chaco culture, and the mysterious cliff dwellings of the thirteenth-century Mogollon tribe. Mexican Pueblo settlements of sun-baked adobe structures and the abandoned communities of silver miners and gold prospectors are further reminders of the cultural diversity of the region.

Navajos believe that they have journeyed through several other worlds to this life, and have always considered the land in the Southwest to be sacred. Many descendants of area tribes now live on reservations, which occupy half the states' lands.

A reliable water supply has transformed the once desolate, forbidding desert into an attractive option for transplanted telecommuters, immigrants, and retirees. Indeed, the dry air, endless sunshine, and world-class golf courses have placed Phoenix, Albuquerque, and Tucson among the country's fastest-growing communities.

Billions of years of evolution, severe wind and water erosion, and geographical anomalies reveal themselves in dramatic fashion in some of the area's natural features. The rainbow-striped rock of the Painted Desert, the red sandstone monoliths of Monument Valley, the purple-hued Grand Canyon, and the bleached landscape of White Sands Monument all give lie to the idea that desert scapes come in two monotonous tones of brown.

The South

(Virginia, West Virginia, Kentucky, Tennessee, North Carolina, South Carolina, Florida, Georgia, Alabama, Mississippi, Central Texas, Arkansas, Louisiana, and parts of Missouri and Oklahoma.)

> "Dum spiro, spero" ("While I breathe, I hope")
> *State motto of South Carolina*

Forged by its history, climate, and location and expressed in music, food, and the drawl of its accent, the South possesses perhaps the strongest regional personality. From the Civil War to the civil rights movement, from huge territorial acquisitions to the constant stream of immigrants, the South has been shaped by its diversity, its turbulent past, and the ongoing challenge of social integration. The conflicts—both physical and political—have created a fiercely independent spirit. While Texas is characterized as having a devil-may-care nature, the rest of the South is known for its hospitality, charm, and gentle pace.

The old Mason-Dixon line, which demarcated north from south in the late 1700s, may have been erased from the maps, but a strong divide still exists, as witnessed in South Carolina's controversial battle to keep the Confederate flag. The unofficial motto of the Lone Star state—"Don't mess with Texas"—reminds us that this state was once independent, and still considers itself to be a republic!

This broad sweep of states is a study in contrasts and superlatives. The ostentatious affluence of such cities as Charleston and Atlanta contrasts sharply with Mississippi shantytowns and West Virginia trailer parks. The region embraces the highlands of Missouri's Ozark, Virginia's Blue Ridge, and Tennessee's Great Smoky Mountains, as well as the fertile cotton belt of the interior plain. A scattering of hurricane-weary coastal islands dots the lower eastern seaboard. The delicate ecosystem of the Florida Everglades sustains the sly alligator and the strange-looking manatee. Among the most evocative images of the South are the mangrove swamps and the Spanish moss dripping from ancient oaks in Louisiana bayou country.

Alaska and Hawaii
Adding to the nation's geographical diversity are the glacial mountains of Alaska, featuring

America's highest peak, Mount McKinley. A tourist's paradise, the Hawaiian islands boast volcanic formations, tropical vegetation, and the occasional black sand beach.

A NATION OF IMMIGRANTS

> **"E Pluribus Unum" ("Out of many, one")**
> *America's first national motto*

For the English seeking religious freedom, Jews fleeing pogroms in Eastern Europe, and Irish escaping famine, America represented a land of refuge and opportunity. The Statue of Liberty provided the first glimpse of America and a symbol of hope for the millions of people who arrived in New York harbor.

The museum on neighboring Ellis Island, the site of the original immigration-processing center, chronicles the experiences, hardships, and eventual settlement patterns of America's newcomers. Today, approximately 40 percent of Americans are descendants of the 12 million people, most of them Europeans, who entered the U.S.A. through Ellis Island between its peak years of 1892 and 1954.

America's ethnic tapestry has always been a work in progress. According to the 2000 Census, the U.S. population is currently composed of 1.5 percent Native American Indian and Alaskans, 13 percent Hispanic, 13 percent African-American, and 4 percent Asian. The remaining 68.5 percent identified their race as "white," although this figure includes many of mixed race.

While whites are distributed throughout the country, minorities tend to be more geographically concentrated. African-Americans live predominantly in the South and in the cities of the industrial Midwest and Northeast. Not surprisingly, Hispanics are heavily concentrated in the southern border states (accounting for 94 percent of the population of Laredo, Texas, for example). The Asian community, one of the fastest-growing demographics, has, for the most part, settled closer to their ports of entry on the West Coast.

The current birthrate is less than 1 percent and an aging population coupled with a dwindling Social Security fund is a matter of concern for America's politicians and employers alike. However, immigration continues to boost the population by about a million every year. Hispanics (who have a higher than average birthrate) have overtaken African-Americans as the fastest-growing ethnic group. Illegal immigrants are estimated to number 11 million, and pose a variety of social, political, and economic challenges.

If current patterns continue, the U.S. population is projected to reach 409 million in 2050, with whites making up 52 percent of the population, African-Americans 13 percent, Hispanics 25 percent, and Asians 10 percent.

Just as the face of America is changing, so are ideologies on how to integrate immigrants. Newcomers are no longer expected to plunge into the "all-American stew." The new ideal is a society that promotes respect for cultural difference while promising equality for all. Visitors to an immigrant community are likely to see individuals adept at navigating two cultural worlds. By day, people from diverse backgrounds operate harmoniously in mainstream American society. At day's end, however, they return home and seamlessly revert to their own language, traditions, and cultural identity.

The Melting Pot

An early mention of the melting pot philosophy appears in Israel Zangwill's 1908 play, *The Melting Pot*: "Germans, Frenchmen, Irishmen, Englishmen, Jews and Russians . . . into the crucible with you all! God is making the American!"

The national character has always been defined—and challenged—by immigration. Like a kaleidoscope, as immigrants from an increasingly wide range of countries enter the picture, the pattern of American society as a whole changes. Further, as newcomers add their own version of a strong work ethic and family values to the mix, America's founding principles of inclusion and diversity are not only strengthened, but made more relevant and dynamic.

GOVERNMENT

The United States' system of government was established in 1789, based on the world's first written constitution (1787). The Constitution designed a system of checks and balances that would protect Americans against excessive central power. It separated the government into three branches—executive, legislative, and judicial— and balanced power between the federal government and the individual states.

A Bill of Rights (added to the Constitution in 1791) protects individual liberties from the long arm of government. Considered one of the cornerstones of American democracy, it includes the right to free speech, the right to bear arms, and the right not to incriminate oneself.

The ever-shifting distribution of powers between the different branches of government is a constant source of controversy. Applying the sometimes ambiguous words of the 200-year-old Constitution to today's societal challenges provides job security for constitutional scholars and Supreme Court justices alike. Yet few would dispute that the document is remarkable in having articulated the values and aspirations of successive generations of Americans since 1788.

The Executive
The executive branch of government consists of a president and a vice president (who are elected "on the same ticket" for four years), and a cabinet composed of the heads (or secretaries) of the fifteen executive departments. The president serves as head of state and head of the armed forces, and is restricted to a maximum of two elected terms in office.

The Legislature
The bicameral legislative branch of government (Congress) comprises two houses: the 100-member Senate, and the 435-member House of Representatives. The number of congressmen and women elected to the House of Representatives

from each state is based on its population. Members serve two-year terms. In the Senate, each state is represented by two members. Senators serve six-year terms, with one-third of the seats being up for election every two years.

The Judiciary
The judicial branch of government is headed by the Supreme Court of nine judges, who are appointed for life by the president. The highest court in the land, it is the final arbiter in determining the constitutionality of legislative and executive actions and maintaining the balance between state and federal institutions.

The States
With the passage of time, the delicate balance of power has shifted away from the states, as the role of central government has steadily expanded. The individual states still retain significant administrative and policy-making autonomy, however.

The visitor can be baffled by the wide variance in state laws, with everything from drinking age to capital punishment being adjudicated by geography. Most states replicate the federal structure, each having its own constitution, a chief executive (the governor), a bicameral state congress, and a judiciary.

Political Parties

The "winner take all" electoral structure favors a two-party system. Democrats tend to be more liberal than Republicans, and believe in a stronger role for government. They countenance higher taxes to pay for social programs. Regarded as "the party of the people," the Democratic party has particular appeal to ethnic minorities and women.

Considered to be more socially conservative and pro free enterprise than the Democrats, the Republican party favors state rights and strengthening the armed forces. Republicans count a strong following among the middle class, business interests, and the farming community.

By European standards, both are fairly centrist and party lines are frequently crossed when voting on legislation. In fact, politicians often demonstrate more loyalty to the agenda of their home constituents than that of their party. Another significant feature of the political scene is the special interest groups that lobby politicians to influence their policy decisions.

Federal Electoral System

Presidential elections are held every four years, on the first Tuesday in November. The inauguration of the winning candidate is held on the following January 20.

Confusing to many outsiders, technically the president is elected not by universal suffrage but by a 538-member electoral college. How does this work? Each state has a number of electoral-college votes, proportionate to the size of its population. When people vote for a presidential candidate, they are actually instructing their state electoral college to cast their votes for that candidate. The candidate who receives the most votes is awarded that state's entire allocation of electoral-college votes. The presidency is awarded to the candidate who receives a majority of the nation's 538 electoral-college votes.

One repercussion of the 2000 election, in which George W. Bush lost the popular vote but won the presidency, has been to focus attention on whether this system truly expresses the will of the people.

THE USA: A BRIEF HISTORY

Despite the presence of indigenous Amerindian tribes and evidence of a tenth-century Viking settlement in Newfoundland, the official title of "discoverer of America" (with accompanying national holiday) is generally conferred upon the Italian explorer Christopher Columbus. In one of the most profitable navigational mistakes in history, in 1492 Columbus mistook the Caribbean islands for the spice-rich East Indies, and its native people for "Indians."

As tales of spectacular abundance reached the shores of Europe, the race to colonize the New World got under way. The Spanish claimed large tracts of the South and Southwest. The French focused on fur trading further north. Interestingly, most of the land on the eastern seaboard, today's most populous region, was considered to be mosquito ridden and uninhabitable. An entire island colony (Roanoke) established by Walter Raleigh off the Carolinas mysteriously disappeared. British luck changed when tobacco became Europe's new addiction. A colony was founded at Jamestown in 1607 to produce the cash crop for the British crown. By the mid 1700s, British settlers had established thirteen colonies on the east coast stretching from Maine to Georgia.

A Model Society

One of these was Plymouth Colony in modern-day Massachusetts, founded by the Puritans, a fundamentalist Protestant sect that had fled persecution by the Church of England. Their leader, John Winthrop, envisioned their self-governing community as a "model society" in a new land. From the Puritans, America inherited the ideal that this great experiment in nation building was to be an example, a "shining city upon a hill" for other countries to look up to.

Competing European ambitions in the new country led to the Seven Years' War (1757–63), resulting in England claiming Canada and all of North America east of the Mississippi. Victorious but smarting from the expense of maintaining its colonies, the English authorities decided to raise American taxes. In response, the colonists united behind a banner of "No Taxation without Representation" and, knowing just how to upset the British, dumped consignments of highly taxed tea into Boston Harbor.

Revolution and Independence

Antitax protests escalated and tensions mounted, but the first shots were not fired until April 19, 1775, when British soldiers confronted colonial rebels in Lexington, Massachusetts, and the American Revolution was under way.

On July 4, 1776, the leaders of the thirteen colonies, finally united by a common cause, signed a Declaration of Independence providing for self-determination (and a perfect excuse for an annual barbecue). Full independence was secured five years later following the English surrender at Yorktown, Virginia (1781).

Birth of a Nation
The "Articles of Confederation," the wartime manifesto drafted to unite the colonies, was deemed inadequate to address the post-Revolution challenges of governing the country. Summoned to Philadelphia in 1787 to revise it, the state delegates (later immortalized as the nation's "Founding Fathers") preferred to start with a blank slate—a metaphor for the newly independent country. The result was the U.S. Constitution, a document that has provided the political and legal framework for the country since its ratification in 1788. The following year, George Washington became the first U.S. President.

Manifest Destiny
Having rid itself of colonial overlords, America turned its attention westward. In 1803 President Thomas Jefferson purchased the Louisiana

Territory from the cash-strapped Napoleon. This doubled the country's size, pushed the boundaries as far west as the Rockies, and gave access to the Mississippi waterway. By mid-century, a series of territorial wars and land treaties had added the present-day states of Oregon, Washington, Texas, New Mexico, Arizona, California, Utah, and Colorado to the union.

Americans believed it was their "manifest destiny" to settle all parts of North America. However, as an increasing number of settlers, gold prospectors, and cattle drivers pushed west, the fate of the Native Americans, who had long inhabited the lands, was manifestly sealed. Throughout the 1800s, Native Americans were dispossessed of their land through a serious of spurious land deals, government deceptions, and bloody conflicts. The Indian Removal Act (1830) forcibly relocated tribes from their southeastern homelands to designated "Indian Territory" in Oklahoma. The route traveled and the journey itself was evocatively immortalized as the "Trail of Tears."

Later, the influx of settlers attracted to free government land by the Homestead Act (1862) sparked clashes with the Great Plains tribes. Called in to protect the new farming settlements, the U.S. army fought a series of wars with the Cheyenne, Arapaho, and Sioux between 1862 and and 1876. The battles included the last U.S. military defeat

THE NATIVE AMERICANS

Territorial wars, disease, and confinement to government reservations reduced the Native American population from an estimated 4.5 million at the onset of European colonization to 350,000 by 1920.

Today, after several missteps, government, society—even Hollywood—acknowledge the wrongs perpetrated in the rush to settle America. Unemployment, illiteracy, and poverty remain challenges among Native Americans. Yet they have demonstrated a great resilience of spirit: according to the 2000 Census, Native Americans now number about three million. Many have made unique contributions to American society while continuing to honor their cultural heritage.

Visitors to the Southwest or Plains states can best learn about the Native American culture and way of life by listening, observing—and leaving the cameras at home.

on American soil, when Custer's "last stand" was overrun by the Sioux at Little Big Horn. Today, a monument to Chief Crazy Horse in South Dakota recognizes him as a symbol of the resistance and heartbreak of the Indian nations.

The Civil War

The "peculiar institution" of slavery started in the early 1600s when Africans were forcibly transported to the United States and sold at auction to replace poor whites and Native Americans as "indentured servants." As the agricultural economy developed in the South, between 1619 and 1865 three million slaves were brought to the United States to labor on Southern tobacco, sugar cane, and cotton plantations.

Slavery drove a deep wedge into the existing political and economic divisions between the North and South. The farms and industries of the populous Northern states had less need for slaves and abolished the practice in 1804. Congress outlawed the import of slaves into the U.S.A. after 1808—but individual states could determine their own policies on the continued trading and "employment" of slaves. As, one by one, newly admitted western states chose to join the North in becoming "free states," the South felt the political and economic tide shifting against them.

In opposing slavery, the North claimed the moral high ground. The South countered that the very fabric of its economy and society was at stake. When antislavery crusader Abraham Lincoln was elected President (1860), the Southern states defiantly announced they were seceding from the union and forming a Confederacy.

The four-year Civil War was an uneven contest. The industrial North had the advantage in manpower, sophisticated communications, and manufacturing infrastructure. The agrarian south had fine military leaders and a steely resolve—but defeated by Sherman's victory in Atlanta (1864) and subsequent march across the South, the Confederate states surrendered in 1865. Slavery was formally abolished throughout the U.S.A. in 1866. The Civil War was possibly the most tragic chapter in America's short history. It left 600,000 dead. Lincoln never got to savor victory—he was assassinated before the war's final shots were fired.

The Industrial Age

The wounded South struggled with reconstruction, a devastated economy, and a new social order. While slavery was formally abolished, emancipated slaves and their descendants continued to face hardship, segregation, and discrimination.

Fortunes were very different in the North. Here the industrial revolution transformed the U.S.A. into a major economic power. A new breed of business magnate, including J. P. Morgan, John D. Rockefeller, and Andrew Carnegie, built vast empires in banking, oil, and steel. America's new elite, they amassed great wealth and built opulent mansions. Claiming they were merely the "stewards of God's wealth" on earth (and also mindful of antitrust legislation!), they established America's generous tradition of philanthropy.

The late nineteenth century also brought a significant change in the demographic makeup. Adding to the steady stream of English, Irish, German, and Dutch, immigrants from Central Europe flocked to work in the Northeast's factories, and the Chinese descended on California's gold mines. Meanwhile, rapid industrialization created new social challenges. The middle-class activism of the Progressive Movement brought about laws to improve living and working conditions, address workers' rights, and regulate business.

Revolutionary advances in transportation and communication technology helped integrate the country, at the same time opening it up to new possibilities. The transcontinental railroad (1869), for example, carried western beef and wheat to the east, and settlers and manufactured goods back west. As the developing country sprawled out, American cities began to rise up, as Louis Sullivan's steel-framed "skyscrapers" carved out Manhattan's legendary skyline.

An End to Isolationism
Having populated its interior and established itself as an economic power, America decided to

expand its influence overseas. Alaska had been purchased from Russia in 1867. Victory in the Spanish-American War (1898) allowed the U.S.A. to expand its influence into the Caribbean and Pacific with the acquisition of Guam, the Philippines, and Puerto Rico, and control over Cuba. It further expanded its empire by annexing the sugar-producing islands of Hawaii (1898), and opening up the Panama Canal (1914).

It has been noted that, when it came to U.S. commercial expansionism, the dollar has never been "isolationist." When it came to the military and political affairs of other countries, however, America had long pursued the isolationist stance outlined by President Monroe in 1823. This ended in 1917, three years into the First World War, when the German decision to attack neutral shipping prompted President Wilson to enter the conflict. The massive injection of American troops to bolster the depleted Allied ranks was decisive in securing peace in November, 1918.

Policeman of the World

President Theodore Roosevelt first envisioned the role of the "world's policeman" for the U.S.A. in the early 1900s. He advocated a policy of deterrence through military preparedness when he cautioned, "Speak softly, and carry a big stick."

The Great Depression

The 1920s were boom years for the economy, with America acquiring the taste for mass consumption of mass-produced goods. When Henry Ford first introduced his Model T car to the country, it was love at first sight. With the advent of Hollywood motion pictures, images of the "American Dream" were exported around the world.

But the unchecked growth of the economy led to rampant speculation. On October 24, 1929, the stock market collapsed, plunging the nation into the Great Depression. Many lost their businesses and life savings. Farmers weren't spared, as a drought destroyed crops and livelihoods. Roosevelt's New Deal policies provided relief—but recovery was agonizingly slow.

The Second World War

American isolationism was tested once again when Britain declared war on the German Nazi regime. Recalcitrance ended with the Japanese attack on Pearl Harbor, Hawaii, on December 7, 1941, propelling America overnight into the Second World War. The war in Europe ended in May, 1945, but raged on in the Pacific until August, when the U.S. dropped atomic bombs on Japan, at Hiroshima and Nagasaki. America justified the action by saying the alternative, an invasion of Japan, would have incurred greater losses on both sides.

The Cold War

If anyone was in any doubt, the establishment of the
Marshall Plan (1947) and the creation of NATO
(1949), committing American capital and troops to
the reconstruction and defense of a democratic
Europe, signaled a clear end to U.S. isolationism.

The rapid spread of totalitarian regimes in
postwar Eastern Europe and the Communist
takeover in China alarmed Americans.
Playing up the paranoia to justify his
"Communist containment" foreign
policy, President Truman ordered
Senator Joseph McCarthy to
investigate and expose all
"Communist subversives" living on American soil.

Concerns over expanding Communist influence
in Asia led to U.S. military intervention in Korea
(1950–53) and later Vietnam (1964–75). The
competition between the Soviets and Americans
for the mantle of "superpower" also resulted in a
dangerous proliferation of atomic and later
nuclear weapons. In 1962, in one of the most
serious confrontations, President Kennedy ordered
the Soviets to remove nuclear missiles from Cuban
bases. After a tense standoff, Russia's President
Khrushchev backed down, and nuclear war was
averted. A grateful nation was grief-stricken the
following year when the popular young President
was assassinated by a Soviet sympathizer.

The Turbulent Sixties

The era of postwar nationalism had ended. The sixties were characterized by traumatic upheaval. America's growing involvement in the Vietnam War polarized the nation, which became increasingly convinced that stemming the Communist tide half a world away was no justification for the loss of 58,000 American lives. Under mounting pressure, President Nixon signed a peace treaty with North Vietnam in 1973. The returning troops met with an indifferent reception; it wasn't until 1982 that wounds had healed sufficiently to erect the Vietnam War Memorial, honoring the fallen.

Back home, Dr. Martin Luther King Jr. became the leader and the lightning rod for the Civil Rights movement. He was assassinated in 1968, the same year as another social activist, Senator Robert Kennedy. President Lyndon Johnson later enacted legislation to end racial segregation.

The sixties "counterculture" also produced advances in the rights of women, homosexuals, and immigrant workers. The tumultuous decade ended with a rare moment of unity when, in 1969, the U.S.A. successfully landed a man on the moon.

Watergate to Whitewater

His significant foreign policy achievements overshadowed by the Watergate scandal, disgraced President Nixon resigned in 1974. Despite the success of President Jimmy Carter (1976–80) in securing the Camp David Egyptian-Israeli peace agreement, the energy crisis and the American hostage drama in Iran sank his administration. The two terms of the popular President Reagan (1980–88) were characterized by a conservative social agenda, foreign policy incursions, and deficit-inducing tax cuts.

The early 1990s witnessed a return to military intervention overseas, as Iraq's invasion of Kuwait prompted George Bush Senior to unleash the technological warfare of Desert Storm. Victorious abroad, Bush was defeated in 1992 by Bill Clinton, who was able to capitalize on domestic challenges. Despite being dogged by scandal, Clinton had solid public support throughout his two terms, buoyed primarily by a booming economy.

War on Terrorism
The U.S.A. entered the twenty-first century as the world's only superpower—but with a new, faceless foe. The devastating terrorist attacks of September 11, 2001, which killed 2,800 people on American soil, resulted in U.S. military intervention in Afghanistan and Iraq. Once again, with one eye on international events and the other looking for "the enemy within," this nation of immigrants is challenged to uphold its founding ideals of equality, justice, and liberty.

VALUES &
ATTITUDES

What really matters to Americans? It might seem impossible to generalize across vast distances and a population of 290 million who are renowned for being highly individualistic. Yet the special character and unique experiences of the early settlers and successive waves of immigrants have indeed shaped a set of all-American values.

AMERICA—THE IDEAL

In his 1995 book *American Exceptionalism*, Seymour Lipset observes that America is the only nation in the world that is founded on a creed. Unlike societies where nationality is related to birthright, becoming an American is more of a conscious act, an ideological commitment to a set of values and a way of life.

Despite their different backgrounds or motivations, those who came willingly to America were bound together by similar beliefs, united in the same mission. They rejected notions of a state-mandated religion, a powerful centralized government, or a rigid class structure. Their utopian ideal was to have the space and freedom to create a model society. They believed that morality and hard work led to the improvement of mankind and the betterment of society. Everyone had an equal chance of success because every individual was free to control his own destiny. These guiding principles of liberty, equality—even the "pursuit of happiness"—were modeled and reinforced by colonial America's early leaders. Later institutionalized in the Declaration of Independence and the Constitution, they have shaped public policy and national values ever since.

IN GOD WE TRUST

Today the fact that millions of immigrants still clamor for U.S. citizenship reinforces the nation's conviction that America is still, as Lincoln described it, "the last, best hope on earth."

EQUALITY OF OPPORTUNITY

Early on, Americans were determined to make their new society a meritocracy. First enshrined in the Declaration of Independence, the phrase "all men are created equal" emphasized that, regardless of race, religion, or background, every individual should be provided with equal opportunity to succeed. Rungs on the ladder of success would not be arbitrarily allocated by birthright, but achieved through initiative and perseverance.

Equal opportunity is not to be confused with egalitarianism (another important American value). In his book *Democracy in America* (1835) de Tocqueville first observed that emphasis is placed on equality of *opportunity*—not *equal conditions* for all. Consistent with their individualistic mentality, Americans believe that ability, effort, and achievement should be rewarded, and reject the notion of government interference to iron out social and economic inequities. Rather than investing in a European-style welfare state, America "levels the playing field" and promotes upward mobility by making its educational system flexible and accessible to all.

"I DID IT MY WAY"

The right to control your own destiny is a cherished American value. Individual rights and freedoms are fiercely defended. While the conformist Japanese warn that "the nail that sticks up gets hammered down," Americans believe that "the squeaky wheel gets the grease." In other words, speak up, get yourself noticed, and you'll get your needs met.

The nation's greatest admiration is reserved for

those iconic individuals who have blazed new trails—pioneering aviator Charles Lindbergh, for example—or those who have made a difference by standing up for their beliefs, such as the slain civil rights leader Dr. Martin Luther King Jr.

How can a nation of individualists also be team players? The American notion of "group" or "team" affiliation is different from that of collectivist countries. While fully committed to the team's goal, individuals will also use group membership to advance a personal agenda—to showcase their talents. Once the group no longer serves the individual's purpose, it's time to end the association and move on to the next opportunity, "no strings attached." From the conference room to the locker room, individual members will expect to be rewarded based on individual contribution, with the star player receiving the lion's share. It's fun to be a part of a team and great things can be achieved together, but at the end of the day you have to "look out for number one."

An "I" Society
A keyword search for book titles containing the word "self" revealed 154,552 titles, including *Self Matters* and *How to Be Your Best Self*. While not all were written by Americans, it is a safe bet that 153,000 probably were!

In what Lipset dubbed the "double-edged sword" of American values, positive traits, when taken to extreme, can become negative influences. The Constitution's emphasis on individual rights was originally designed to protect citizens against government abuse of power. Today, the media gives the impression that Americans sue each other at the drop of a hat, clogging the court systems and enriching the country's lawyers. Some wonder if the threat of litigation has replaced personal responsibility and common sense. However, it should be noted that individual or "class action" lawsuits often result in significant public policy change—antismoking and drunk-driving legislation, for example—making the country safer for all through individual initiative.

SELF-RELIANCE

Stemming from individualism and the hardships and isolation endured by early settlers, Americans value self-reliance. Bennet and Stewart (*American Cultural Patterns*) quote examples from the myths of the Wild West, such as the lone cowboy or frontiersman who single-handedly imposed justice on outlaws. Today's mythic loners, they suggest, are the "lonely detective or irate citizen who challenge the system and impose law and order personally."

Clearly, the notion that "God helps those who help themselves" inspired the American work ethic in its early years. This has evolved into a mentality of "self-help" in seeking solutions to modern-day challenges. Good American parents instill this value by offering their children every opportunity to prepare for adulthood, then launching them out of the nest to make their own way in the world. Elderly people prefer to remain self-reliant, too. They would rather live in a retirement community or nursing home than become dependent on family members. In the same vein, practical assistance is given to the physically or mentally disabled to allow them to lead independent lives and develop their full potential.

VOX POPULI

In colonial America, populism took root as local citizens met in town halls to discuss community issues. Antagonism toward a distant colonial authority that imposed rule from the top down inspired Americans to create a system that would work from the grass roots up—a government "of the people, by the people."

Today, more public offices are elected positions, and elections and referendums are held more often, than in any other country—the *Economist* estimated about one million in each four-year election cycle! Citizens, local government, or states can propose legislation—as witnessed when California's voters elected to recall their Governor, replacing him with actor Arnold Schwarzenegger.

Then why does a country that cherishes its democratic ideals record such low voter turnout year after year? Lipset suggests that the answer may lie in the frequency of elections, the protracted and negative nature of campaigns, and a two-party system that leaves many to vote simply for the lesser of two evils.

EGALITARIANISM

Consistent with the belief that "all men are born equal," American social relations are founded on equal respect and informality. In an early example of egalitarianism, the Congress of 1789 decided that George Washington should be addressed simply as "Mr. President." Today's corporate CEO is referred to as Jack (or Carly), and the restaurant staff expect to be on first-name terms with you, too.

Is America a classless society? Yes and no. While social stratification does exist, the concept of class is entirely different in America. In the traditional societies of Europe, class denotes an inherited station in life. Here, it is an acquired status—a position earned through effort and achievement. This means that—unlike class—social standing is not defined by accent, affiliations, or geography, but by money and power. The acquisition of a new car or the latest electronic toy may be regarded as rampant materialism by outsiders. To Americans, these are symbols of status and success.

Of course, some have a "leg up" by being born into privilege. But, in theory, anyone can make a million or go to Harvard in this socially mobile society. Indeed, America reveres those who have risen from humble beginnings and overcome adversity to achieve success. There is also far less deference to authority, and fewer privileges based on rank. President or pauper, everyone's expected to stand in line and clear their table at a fast-food restaurant.

WORK ETHIC

The Protestant work ethic provided a clear and compelling equation to early settlers: hard work led to a moral life, spiritual fulfillment, and God's blessing in the form of material rewards here on earth. Benjamin Franklin encapsulated much of the work ethic in *Poor Richard's Almanack* (1736), coining sayings still used today, such as "Early to bed, early to rise, makes a man healthy, wealthy, and wise," and "Time is money." Today, on average, Americans still work three hundred hours a year more than workers in other countries.

Unlike "work to live" cultures, where work is just one of the many dimensions of one's life, for many Americans work is central in defining one's sense of identity and self-worth. Even those who can afford to step off the treadmill often don't. To many, work is an end in itself: the sense of purpose and accomplishment are as much of a reward as the paycheck or pension plan.

In this land of abundance, success did not have to be gained at the expense of others—excepting always the experience of the Native Americans and the slave-owning South. Everyone had the opportunity to work toward a better future. This explains why there is no guilt attached to enjoying the "fruits of one's labors." Early Puritans or Benjamin Franklin might be bemused by some of today's "blessings," such as big screen TVs and designer sneakers, but they would be pleased to see that the work ethic is alive and well!

> "Work: 1. That which keeps us out of trouble.
> 2. A plan of God to circumvent the Devil."
> *The Roycroft Dictionary & Book of Epigrams, 1923*

GIVING BACK

When John F. Kennedy, in his 1960 inaugural address, exhorted Americans, "Ask not what your country can do for you, ask what you can do for your country," he was preaching to the choir. The U.S.A. outstrips every other nation in terms of time and money donated to worthy causes. One in four American adults volunteer their time on a regular basis. The combination of America's generosity and "can do" attitude has produced an industry that contributed 239 billion dollars to the U.S. economy in 2001.

The first volunteer organizations were faith-based groups that assumed responsibility for the social welfare programs usually administered by the government. Today individuals from all walks of life donate privately, or organize charity events through their work, school, or community group. Every weekend thousands run to fight global hunger, or walk to buy a new roof for the local church. Even more telling, busy Americans donate time to help those in need. Volunteers from all backgrounds and ages teach, mentor, and act as information guides: they develop financial plans, serve at soup kitchens, and operate crisis hotlines.

What motivates this constant outpouring of generosity? Americans get to apply their skills and energy, "give back" to the community, and make a difference. In return, conscience, body, and wallet have had a workout, and society has been self-supporting—not reliant on government handouts. It's a win-win proposition for all.

GOOD OR EVIL

Based on exported pop-culture images of fun-loving, midriff-baring teens, visitors to the United States may be surprised at just how moralistic the society is. Reflecting the early Puritan tradition, Americans tend to view morality in absolute terms. Whereas in Europe, abortion and gay rights are regarded as political issues, in the U.S.A. they are defined in moral and ethical terms, often polarizing the nation and provoking emotional debate. As Lipset points out, wars are similarly moralistic crusades—democracy against the evil empire.

The sexual peccadilloes of a president would be irrelevant in Europe. Americans, on the other hand, expect the highest level of moral conduct in the nation's leader (although they will countenance a few jokes at his expense by late-night comedians.) What does all this mean for the tourist? Don't expect to find nude sunbathing on beaches, or sex on network TV.

CHANGE IS GOOD

America was founded by a special breed of adventurous, entrepreneurial types who sought new frontiers to conquer. They found plentiful resources and a young society, people who thought that constant change was a duty, and that progress was its reward.

The "change equals progress" equation has shaped a future-oriented culture that rewards "go getters" who "think out of the box" and "push the envelope." With vision, energy, and perseverance, anything can be accomplished.It is a conviction that has placed a man on the moon, and produced three times as many Nobel prize winners as the next country. It is why the introduction of a globally implemented IT system or a new brand of washing powder is automatically and enthusiastically embraced. If it's new, it must be improved.

Unwavering optimism and faith in the future inspire not only action but a confident swagger and upbeat tone—today is good, but tomorrow can only be better.

CONTROL FREAKS

> "The Yankee means to make moonlight work, if he can."
> *Ralph Waldo Emerson, 1846*

To be in control, it helps to have nature on your side. Some cultures live in harmony with their environment. Americans like to wrestle it to the ground and harness its power for their own personal use. Wind, sun, and ocean waves are transformed into valuable energy sources; state-of-the-art heating and air-conditioning systems allow Alaskans and Floridians to enjoy the same room temperatures all year round.

Fatalistic cultures believe that bad luck is inevitable and destiny is determined by the fickle finger of fate. To Americans, that is superstitious claptrap. Rather than passively reacting to events, Americans take control by being proactive. In her book *The Yin and Yang of American Culture*, Dr. Eun Kim observes that: "Americans are obsessed with controlling their destiny, from health to happiness." They have perfected the art of predicting, diagnosing, and controlling every aspect of life. Is ill health unavoidable? Not if you exercise, take dietary supplements, and engage in preventative medical checks. Do skyscrapers have to topple in earthquakes? Not if you build them on special rollers. Meanwhile, NASA scientists literally fly into the eye of the storm to gather forecasting information to reduce the national impact of deadly hurricanes. Only in America! And if all else fails and the randomness of nature prevails? As Kim notes, that's what insurance policies are for!

TIME IS MONEY
The obsession with control extends to time. Time is money and as such it should be wisely managed and spent, never frittered away. Lawyers bill by the

minute, phone companies by the second, and local news channels boast they can cover international news in one minute flat. "Beating the clock" is less about punctuality and more about organization and efficient use of time. High-tech time-planning tools such as PDAs are the nation's favorite new toys; even the Luddite will have a desktop diary. For the time challenged there are time-management books and courses a-plenty. And what do you do with the time saved? Fill it, of course! As the saying goes, "If you want something done, give it to a busy person." The worst nightmare for the tightly scheduled? "Downtime"—an unexpected delay that leaves you stranded without a laptop, cell phone, or to do list, leading to the ultimate sacrilege of "killing time."

DIVERSITY

Americans proudly assert that "in diversity there is strength," and also challenge. Legislation and increased social awareness have led to greater equality for all, regardless of race, ethnicity, creed, gender, sexual orientation, or disability. Progress may be slow, but changing societal attitudes can be measured in the use of more respectful terminology for minorities, the spread of multilingual signs and services, and corporate initiatives to promote diversity in the workplace.

Affirmative action initiatives, ensuring that employers and educational institutions allocate a designated number of places to minority groups, have attempted to redress injustices in the system. Some people, however, counter that this constitutes "reverse discrimination." Thus the ideal of equality of opportunity continues to bump up against the reality of existing socio-economic inequities and lingering discrimination.

PATRIOTISM

Post-Revolutionary Americans had neither a long shared history nor a common cause to rally around once they had expelled the British. A sense of identity and unity had to be forged. The Constitution and the flag soon became patriotism's most potent symbols.

To the visitor, the American flag seems to be everywhere. It not only flies outside public

buildings but graces many a front lawn. The national anthem is a story about the flag that flew throughout the night during the British bombardment of Baltimore's Fort McHenry in 1812; it represents the strength of the American spirit. Schoolchildren swear allegiance to the flag and when the national anthem plays, people stand, and many place their hands on their hearts.

No other country can equal the number of songs inspired by patriotism, among them "America the Beautiful," "God Bless America," and "You're a Grand Old Flag." Jimi Hendrix even provided the antiestablishment, hippie gathering at the 1969 Woodstock music festival with a searing electric version of America's national anthem.

As guests in America, how should visitors react to the American predilection for wearing their patriotism on their sleeve? By going with the flow, leaving the jaded cynicism at home, and demonstrating a sympathetic understanding of the historical and cultural forces that have shaped the deep sense of national pride.

chapter three

CUSTOMS & TRADITIONS

SEPARATION OF CHURCH AND STATE

At American award ceremonies, tearful Country and Western singers, hip-hop stars, and Oscar winners often thank God in their acceptance speeches. The depth and pervasiveness of spiritual life in America is surprising to many outsiders. Like many aspects of U.S. culture, religion is full of contradictions and paradoxes, New World adaptations of Old World influences, and amazing diversity.

One of the first acts of the fledgling American government was to decree the "separation of church and state," stating that "Congress shall make no law respecting an establishment of religion, or prohibiting the free exercise thereof." In theory, this First Amendment to the Constitution ensured that there would be no official government-backed religion. Individuals were free to observe whatever faith they chose.

In practice, Supreme Court justices constantly struggle to determine what constitutes government meddling in religious matters. One glaring contradiction is that while prayer is not allowed in public schools, students recite the "pledge of allegiance" on a daily basis, which contains the line "one nation under God." Similarly, even though the government is not supposed to endorse any one religion, new sessions of Congress begin with a prayer, and the President ends speeches with "God bless America."

The controversy has been characterized as pitting civic duty against individual conscience— one cherished American value against another. Recently, the battle lines were drawn over the removal of a sculpture inscribed with the ten commandments from a government building, a municipal courthouse. Meanwhile, middle America charges that oversensitivity and political correctness govern many decisions on religious matters. In another highly publicized case, town officials argued that decorating a fir tree standing in a public space in December did not necessarily constitute an endorsement of Christianity. They lost. The Christmas tree came down.

What isn't in dispute is that 90 percent of Americans express some religious affiliation and approximately 70 percent claim to practice their faith actively. Religion has always been a voluntary activity in the U.S.A., so those who practice their faith do so by choice, as a matter of individual conscience. This may account for the high degree of observance, the depth of fundamentalism, and the wide variety of religions. With about 190 active religious sects, religion in the United States is a buyer's market with some 33 million congregants claiming to have jumped ship to a different denomination.

Currently, according to the 2000 Census, the various Protestant denominations together constitute 56 percent of the population. It is worth noting, however, that Protestantism covers a vast spectrum with the formal Episcopalian and severe Lutheran doctrines at one extreme and the exuberant gospel-singing Southern Baptist Churches at the other.

Catholics remains the single largest denomination with 27 percent, despite negative publicity regarding Church hierarchy protection for pedophile priests. Many Catholic families send their children to parochial (Catholic) schools, which offer strict academic and disciplinary standards and the freedom to hold religious services.

Islam, which has attracted many African-American converts, is the fastest-growing religion, recently displacing Judaism as the third-largest religious group, while increasing numbers of

Asian immigrants are boosting the numbers of Buddhist and Hindu congregations.

Most of the country's 5.5 million Jews belong to one of three denominations—Orthodox, Conservative, or Reform, with the Orthodox sect being most observant in terms of diet, lifestyle, and religious practice, and Reform the most liberal. Many Jewish children attend school in the public (government) system but receive religious instruction at a Hebrew school. There are also many nonreligious Jews who still derive a strong sense of identity and community from their Jewish ethnicity.

The climate of tolerance and renewal in America fostered the growth of many new religious movements among early settlers. Surviving examples are the Church of Jesus Christ of Latter Day Saints (Mormons), Seventh Day Adventists, and Jehovah's Witnesses.

One generalization that perhaps *can* be applied is that, throughout its history, Americans of all denominations have regarded the Church as having a major responsibility in building communities, tackling the country's social challenges, and helping society's disenfranchised. Particularly in the Southern states, the local church may play a dominant role in daily life, organizing youth groups, study programs, and social outings. When it comes to volunteering time and money, American generosity is legendary. Many of the country's hungry are fed, the homeless sheltered, and children and elderly people cared for by volunteers from religious institutions.

Some strictly religious sects have remained cohesive, homogeneous communities easily identifiable by their distinctive garb, such as the Amish in Pennsylvania and the Hassidim in New York. By and large, however, visitors should be aware that it is difficult to ascertain either religious affiliation or degree of observance based on appearance and lifestyle. A word of caution: for the most part, Americans are uncomfortable discussing their faith so it should be considered off-limits for conversation.

New Hybrid Religions

Multicultural America has always been adept at adapting and combining the cultural traditions imported by its immigrants. This has created

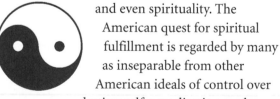

fascinating fusions in cuisine, music, and even spirituality. The American quest for spiritual fulfillment is regarded by many as inseparable from other American ideals of control over destiny, self-actualization, and capacity for reinvention.

Many Americans are no longer monotheistic, instead drawing on traditional belief systems, Eastern philosophies, and New Age practices to create a "pick 'n' mix" approach to fulfilling spiritual and lifestyle needs. Eastern insights are being applied to traditional Judeo-Christian doctrines and new hybrid religions and movements receive celebrity endorsements.

Forms of medicine, exercise, and diet previously thought of as "alternative" are now considered mainstream as yesterday's hippies run today's corporations—or at least the yoga studios and feng shui consultancies.

HATCHED, MATCHED, AND DISPATCHED IN AMERICA
The rituals surrounding births, marriages, and deaths will again be influenced by the religious affiliation, if any, of the participants.

Interfaith marriage is commonplace, and it is not unusual to have a priest and a rabbi coofficiating, or a licensed "marriage celebrant" conducting a secular service. The style of wedding is often a matter of personal taste and budget. The celebration can range from a New-Age barefoot ceremony on a California beach to a ritualized Greek Orthodox service in Chicago, or a designer-clad sophisticated affair at a New York hotel. One thing is universal—it is impossible to keep all family members happy and the wedding plans stress free!

One common American practice is for family, friends, and colleagues to throw a surprise baby or wedding "shower" for an expectant mother or bride-to-be. This involves baby- or wedding-related decorations, games and a cake, and the "showering" of gifts upon the guest of honor.

Some other important rites of passage observed in American life are religious, such as the Christian First Communion and Jewish Bar Mitzvah (for boys) and Bat Mitzvah (for girls). Others, such as the Hispanic Quinceaneros, or fifteenth-birthday girls' parties, are ethnically based. Perhaps the most commonly shared, and fondly remembered, milestone in a young person's life is Prom Night—celebrating high-school graduation at eighteen.

HOLIDAYS—WHAT THEY ARE AND HOW THEY ARE CELEBRATED

While most American holidays are observed nationwide, they are in fact mandated by individual states, and the way in which they are celebrated is influenced by religious affiliation, ethnic background, and regional culture. In practice, most states observe the federal public holidays. Those that fall on a Saturday or Sunday are observed on a Friday and Monday respectively. On official holidays, schools, banks, private businesses, and government offices will be closed. Transportation and other services will operate on a reduced schedule.

Some holidays are uniquely American celebrations, such as Thanksgiving and Independence Day. Others are religious or ethnic festivals that have been imported by immigrants but that have assumed a distinctively American identity. A case in point is St. Patrick's Day, when Americans of all ethnicities place their tongue firmly in cheek, don something green, and claim to be of Irish descent!

A cynic might say that many of these holidays, particularly religious ones, have lost their original meaning and are kept alive by family tradition and Hallmark marketing. Certainly it seems that no sooner has the St. Patrick's Day green beer gone flat than the "Kiss me I'm Irish" hats are replaced by Easter eggs in store windows.

Cynicism aside, no one mounts a parade, loves the razzmatazz, or gets into the spirit of holidays more than Americans. A holiday is an opportunity to exhibit their patriotism, a coming together to reaffirm their identity and unity. On

Memorial Day, Veterans Day, and Presidents' Day, for example, "Old Glory," the American flag, will be much in evidence. Holidays also mark the rhythm of the seasons. Memorial Day and Labor Day "bookend" the summer season (the latter holiday weekend often devoted to frantic back-to-school shopping!).

In addition to national holidays, there are countless other events ranging from small-town celebrations to countywide affairs. Street parades, often headed by majorettes leading a marching band, demonstrate a uniquely American combination of individualism, competition, and team cooperation.

Communities hold festivals to celebrate whatever it is that has put them on the map. Practically every food, dance, and ethnic group is celebrated with a festival. Polka festivals are held in the North, catfish festivals in the South, and German Oktoberfests in practically every state!

The most widely celebrated holidays are listed in the box opposite.

KEY HOLIDAYS AND CELEBRATIONS

New Year's Day	January 1
Martin Luther King Jr. Day	third Monday in January
Valentine's Day	February 14
Presidents' Day	third Monday in February
St. Patrick's Day	March 17
Good Friday and Easter Sunday	dates vary
Memorial Day	fourth Monday in May
Independence Day	July 4
Labor Day	first Monday in September
Columbus Day	second Monday in October
Halloween	October 31
Veterans Day	November 11
Thanksgiving	fourth Thursday in November
Christmas Day	December 25

Valentine's Day—February 14

Historians disagree on who exactly St. Valentine was, but commercial Valentine cards were first sent in the early 1800s by Miss Esther Howland—an American! February 14 has become a day for Americans to give cards, flowers, and candy to the ones they love. It is not a national holiday, but it surpasses even Christmas for the amount of mail it generates. Couples will plan a romantic dinner, and it is the most popular date on which to propose marriage. Cards and gifts are also exchanged between classmates, and parents and their children.

Fourth of July

This quintessentially American holiday commemorates the signing of the U.S. Declaration of Independence on July 4, 1776. America dresses up in the stars and stripes to celebrate its birthday. Everything from T-shirts to tablecloths is in red, white, and blue. Family and friends gather to enjoy barbecues and picnics against a backdrop of outdoor concerts and fireworks. Hot dogs, hamburgers, corn, and apple pie are the patriotic foods of choice.

Halloween—October 31

On Hallowmas (the feast of All Hallows' Eve— originally the pagan festival of Samhain, or "summer's end") people superstitiously left out sweets to appease the souls of the dead, who were rumored to roam the earth the night before All Saints' Day. In its modern-day American incarnation, Halloween is not a national holiday but has become a highly commercialized event. Wholesome suburban homes are transformed into haunted houses complete with spider webs, skeletons, and witches. Children dress up in costumes, teenagers opting for the gruesome and gory while younger ones dress up as their favorite cartoon character or superhero. They will go from house to house "trick or treating"—receiving candy in return for not playing a prank on the homeowner. Adults can't resist the opportunity to throw a party and indulge their fantasy worlds either, although costumes and masks of current politicians and celebrities tend to be favored over ghouls and ghosts.

Thanksgiving—Fourth Thursday in November
Thanksgiving is a uniquely North American holiday, initiated by early settlers to give thanks for the abundant harvest that allowed them to survive. In the busiest travel period of the year, families reunite and enjoy a feast of traditional, indigenous foods, featuring turkey and dressing, cranberry sauce, candied yams, and pumpkin pie. New Thanksgiving traditions have evolved since the days of the Pilgrims, and the meal is usually sandwiched in between the national television broadcasts of the Macy's (New York) Thanksgiving Day parade in the morning, and a college football game in the afternoon (much to the chagrin of the cook!).

Canadians celebrate their own Thanksgiving on the second Monday of October.

Christmas Day—December 25

Christians celebrate the birth of Jesus Christ on December 25, and for some people this may be the only occasion during the year when they attend church. Even the nonreligious may celebrate, decorating their houses, putting up a Christmas tree, and gathering together with family to exchange gifts and enjoy a special dinner. Unlike Thanksgiving when there are few regional adaptations of traditional fare, the Christmas feast is heavily influenced by ethnic origins. Visit four neighboring households and you'll discover that German *pfeffernuesse*, Italian *crostoli*, Southern bread pudding, and American sugar cookies are all considered the traditional Christmas dessert!

Happy Holidays to All

Those from predominantly Protestant or Catholic countries may be puzzled by Americans in movies wishing each other a hearty "happy holidays" against a backdrop of decorated store windows and December snow. Since the country's inception, well before the advent of political correctness, Americans have always respected the many other holidays observed by those of different religions, races, and ethnicities.

In December, for example, Jews celebrate Hanukkah, the eight-day Festival of Lights, and many African-Americans observe Kwanzaa (December 26 to January 1), a period of reflection and thanksgiving. The significant Arabic communities will fast in the daylight hours during the month of Ramadan. For the Russian and Greek Orthodox Church, Easter is the most significant period in the religious year. The High Holy Days in September, which start with Rosh Hashanah (the Jewish New Year) and culminate in Yom Kippur (Day of Atonement), represent the most religious period of the Jewish calendar.

Various nationalities or ethnic groups may also celebrate their own holidays. Mexico's Independence Day, *cinco de mayo* (May 5), is marked with parties and street parades in larger cities, including New York and Los Angeles. Chinese New Year is observed in the Chinatown districts of New York and San Francisco. The French quarter of New Orleans is the scene of decorated floats, elaborate costumes, and round-the-clock partying in celebration of Mardi Gras (or "Fat Tuesday," the beginning of Lent in late February or early March.) Finally, the Gay Pride parade is a colorful annual fixture on New York and San Francisco's calendars.

chapter four

THE AMERICANS AT HOME

AMERICA'S HOMES, SWEET HOMES

In the pioneering days, when the government was offering free land, legend has it that settlers would gallop into the dusty interior and stick a stake in the ground to claim ownership. Americans today may keep one eye on the mortgage rates before "plotting their stake" into a California subdivision—but home ownership remains a big part of the American Dream.

Early American housing reflected the local climate and available materials. Spanish colonists in the Southwest (inspired by Native American structures) built adobe dwellings; New Englanders constructed gabled houses of local wood; wealthy nineteenth-century industrialists favored European stone and marble. The South is an architectural historian's paradise. From the ornate iron balconies of the French quarter in New Orleans to the Spanish antebellum mansions of Mississippi and Georgia, or the sprawling Texan ranch, each is an exercise in adapting imported ethnic influences to the demands of the local terrain and lifestyle.

Today, America has its fair share of subdivisions—housing developments featuring identical homes on well-manicured adjoining plots. Wherever possible, however, styles of homes are expressions of American individuality. A stroll through a suburban neighborhood might reveal a columned Greek revival style sandwiched between a colonial farmhouse and an English Tudor–style property. None may be more than two years old!

Inspired by the wanderlust of their predecessors, Americans move around the country, for college, for work, or just for a change of lifestyle. In an average one-year period, one in five Americans relocates—25 percent move to an entirely new state or region. Books and magazine  articles on "The Hottest Towns" and online relocation wizards allow people to research the best communities for them based on criteria such as schooling, pollution levels, local taxes, and amenities. The goal may be "the pursuit of happiness," but "lifestyle optimizing" tools allow them to control the odds of a favorable outcome.

In terms of domestic migration trends, the population is becoming increasingly urbanized. A nation of farmers no more, just 20 percent live in rural America. The Northeast is losing population while the suburbs of the South continue to gain. City living is characterized by socioeconomic extremes. In New York City, for instance, government-subsidized, low-income housing projects and lavish multimillion-dollar condos coexist on neighboring blocks. Older style housing consists of row houses—townhouses or brownstones of three to four stories, attached on both sides. They may be single-family dwellings, or divided into smaller apartments or studios. Some high-rise apartment buildings have a population the size of a small village. Life for the inhabitants revolves around a five-block radius and the doorman is a master of discretion— knowing all and saying nothing!

In contrast, the suburbs are the bastion of the manicured "yard," basketball hoop, and SUV (replacing the seventies station wagon.) In the warmer, Southern states, smaller condo complexes with communal facilities are popular with retirees and single professionals alike. The rise of "gated communities" reflects a desire for security, convenience, and the instant sense of community that is difficult for the more transient American to achieve.

The new millennium "cocooning" trend, combined with reality TV's makeover mania, is leading Americans to invest more time and

money than ever in their homes. The do-it-
yourself mentality has spawned a huge industry of
books, TV programs, and hangar-sized home
improvement stores. Satisfaction is gained as
much from the process as the end product. A
"fixer upper" will be transformed into a dream
home—then the owners will move on, ready for
the next project.

Don't Fence Me In
The issue of privacy versus openness is a
paradox—particularly when it comes to the
American home. "Lots" or "yards" (gardens) can
be large, and many are not enclosed by the walls,
fences, or hedges so prevalent in other cultures.
Similarly, "window treatments" frame the
window, but the use of European-style net
curtains to screen out nosey neighbors is rare. In
the same vein, first-time visitors to an American
home may be proudly given the full tour; even
walk-in closets and en suite bathrooms are not
considered off-limits. They may also be
encouraged to help themselves to a soda from the
fridge. All this gives an impression of openness.

Yet Americans do value their personal space
and privacy. A Brazilian expatriate who dropped
in on her usually friendly Connecticut neighbors
unannounced got the clear impression she should
have called first. Similarly, while a typical

suburban home features spacious, communal areas, such as an open-plan kitchen and family room or "den," ample private space is also allowed in the floor plan. A visit to a family home in the evening would likely find the family members dispersed, each independently watching TV, on the phone, surfing the Internet, or otherwise recharging the batteries in the privacy of their own bedroom.

American individualism, expansiveness, and abundance are expressed in lifestyle. Despite the fact that the average household size has declined over the past thirty years from 3.1 people to 2.6 people per household, the average size of a new family home increased during the same period from 1,500 to 2,200 square feet.

A common observation is just how outsized everything is. The beds are king-sized, the TVs have giant screens, the burgers are "whoppers," appliances are "industrial" size. The largest popcorn or soda at the movies can be "supersized." Closets are "walk-in," and some cars are the size of a military vehicle.

THE BLENDED FAMILY
What does an American family look like? A mosaic that slowly but constantly shifts as demographic patterns and attitudes change.

Couples are getting married later (average age twenty-eight for a man, twenty-six for a woman), if at all. Half of all marriages end in divorce, which is probably why increasing numbers prefer to live together without taking the trip down the aisle. Advances in medical technology are allowing women to have children later. One third of American children are born outside marriage. More than half of Americans are—or will be at some point—in a "blended" family situation with stepchildren or parents. Gay couples can adopt children and gain legal recognition of their life partner in many American states.

The birthrate, having declined, has now stabilized, while life expectancy has increased. By the year 2025 it is estimated that one in five Americans will be over sixty-five. This means that the baby-boom generation has to care and plan simultaneously for parents and children.

Only a quarter of America's households is made up of married couples with children—a number slightly surpassed by the number of singles living alone.

In families with two parents, gender equality has reached the boardroom—and the kitchen. The number of dual-earner couples is on the rise—and so is the number of stay-at-home dads.

Despite these trends, surveys show that most Americans still consider family to be the ideal, the bedrock of society. So how has society coped with the seismic shifts of the last century? Americans are rising to the challenge with their customary tolerance, adaptability, and resourcefulness. Creative solutions involving alliances of grandparents, stepparents, single parents, and babysitters make complex family situations work. Statistics show that the combination of smaller families and labor-saving devices means that while working parents may be guilt-ridden, they are actually spending more "quality time" with their children than any previous generation.

Child Rearing

Visitors from cultures where children are raised to be seen but not heard can be shocked at the amount of consultation and negotiation between American parents and their children. The American family is a democracy. Relatively young children are included in family decisions—from choosing burgers or spaghetti for lunch to Florida or California for vacation. Youngsters will usually dictate what they eat, wear, and how they spend their time at an earlier age than in other societies.

Everyone has a right to be heard—no matter how young. This means that parents can be interrupted or a teacher's statement challenged. Such behavior might be deemed disrespectful in a hierarchical society. To individualistic Americans it is a simple matter of expressing an opinion, being an active learner, and exercising their rights. Authority figures do not merit automatic deference, but should earn respect through their actions. Teachers should not be placed on a pedestal, but rather be partners in learning. Parents should be able to answer the question "but why?" rationally. "Because I said so," doesn't cut it. When it comes to discipline, physically reprimanding a child with a smack is severely frowned upon. Parents encourage children to mediate the sandbox skirmishes for him or herself. "Use your words," they are taught.

Both the educational system and home life instill values of independence, self-reliance, and self-expression. This ethos is first displayed in kindergarten in "show and tell," where children build confidence and self-esteem by talking about an interest or achievement to classmates. Rather than rote learning, the emphasis is on teaching children educational self-sufficiency through research, analysis, and problem-solving skills. A percentage of class grade, from first grade to graduate school, is based on class participation, rewarding students for speaking up and "making their mark."

Independence is learned in a series of time-honored steps, as responsibility is gradually meted out. Children as young as six will go on "sleepovers" at each other's houses. Schools and civic and private organizations provide many opportunities for outward-bound weekend or summer camps. The ultimate sign of independence is "getting wheels." In many states, teens can drive at sixteen or seventeen. Driving is considered so important that most schools offer driver education.

Outsiders who judge American society based on media images may be critical of the amount of freedom given to teens. The philosophy is to empower the individual by preparing them with practical information and a sense of moral responsibility. Rather than shield a child from the world, they should be allowed to take risks. The greatest learning, after all, comes from one's mistakes.

Schools play their part, usually providing a comprehensive health education program that also incorporates civic responsibility. In light of tragic school shootings often perpetrated by youngsters who "didn't fit in," a recent focus has been on raising sensitivity to peer pressure, bullying, and the cliquish nature of larger high schools, where "nerds," "goths," and "jocks" are powerful subcultures.

EDUCATION

Like many other aspects of American life, the people refuse to let the government control education. Expatriate families are often shocked to discover that there is no national education system. Most school funding is at the state level, and each district has an elected board of education to set curriculum and handle administration. According to Dr. Anne Copeland, coauthor of *Understanding American Schools*, standards vary so widely that the quality of local schooling often determines where families choose to live.

While the vast majority of children attend public (state-run) schools, many parents look to alternative options, such as independent (private) schools or home schooling. There are also schools with religious affiliations, such as Jewish or Catholic parochial schools, where students can receive the religious instruction forbidden in public schools.

Extracurricular activities are considered an integral part of a child's overall education. Through participation in music, sports, science, arts, and community-service activities, children broaden their horizons and learn new skills.

Similarly, the work ethic kicks in early. With that first roadside lemonade stand, American children of all backgrounds get a taste for financial independence. This often starts with them doing basic household chores in exchange for an allowance (pocket money), continues in the form of a "paper route" or babysitting job, and progresses to a weekend position at a local store or restaurant.

Some claim that all these activities lead to stressed-out families and children who are too tightly scheduled. However, American children seem to thrive by keeping busy and are often well prepared to meet the demands and responsibilities of adult life.

Higher Education
A combination of government loans, scholarships, and grants, together with various means of practical support, encourages students from all walks of life to continue their studies. Indeed, America boasts a higher proportion of higher education students than any other country.

The system focuses on breadth rather than depth of education, with students selecting a "major" field of study in the third year of a four-year degree. American education is also characterized by its flexibility—course credits earned can be switched to a different college, or applied to a different major.

Back to School
"College," "University," even "School," are terms used somewhat interchangeably.

So why does a country that spends more than most industrialized nations on education trail world rankings in academic achievement tests? The answer may lie in its heterogeneity, and the sheer numbers that pass through the system. Educators would also point out that real specialization in the U.S.A. is only expected at the graduate level. America is home to many of the world's most prestigious graduate schools.

Another distinctive feature of the education system is the high cost of tuition. Of America's 3,600 higher education institutions, approximately half are private. A degree from one of the eight "Ivy League" (private) universities may be considered a passport for life, but the pursuit of excellence comes at a cost—about $37,000 for a four-year degree. This explains why many families start saving for college before

Junior has uttered his or her first word. Many students have to be self-supporting, working their way through college, or taking out a student loan. This means that many graduate with a degree— and a heavy debt burden.

THE DAILY GRIND

Just as there are many family structures, so there are new, flexible work arrangements. For some, the daily commute involves an hour in bumper-to-bumper traffic. For "telecommuters," it means navigating the kids' toys to get from the kitchen to the home office. Companies eager to retain high-performing employees are offering on-site childcare facilities, flexible schedules, paternity leave, and work-from-home options.

While 60 percent of women are working, those who choose to be stay-at-home moms are likely to be equally busy—juggling car pooling, community volunteering, further education, exercising, home improvement projects, and countless other activities.

Meals are often eaten on the run—at the desk, in the car, or in front of the TV. Dinner time may be the only opportunity for families to gather and catch up on the day's events. Discussions may range from world news to the status of a homework project. The food may be take-out

Chinese or Italian, something from the freezer, or a home-cooked dinner.

Time is precious, the day is tightly scheduled, and disruptions are unwelcome. Friends and family usually call first before dropping by. Telephone calls may be screened or picked up by an answering machine—in this way family members can return calls at their convenience, and avoid the inevitable dinnertime telemarketer call! As e-mail and voice mail blur the lines further between work and leisure time, evenings are often spent on the phone or computer, or figuring out what needs to be added to tomorrow's to-do list.

For convenience, grocery shopping is often done in bulk on a weekly basis at large supermarkets. The newcomer will be either amused or overwhelmed by the amount of choice, with entire aisles devoted to breakfast cereals or pasta sauce. Store hours vary enormously. Smaller stores open from 9:00 a.m. to 6:00 p.m. Suburban supermarkets often stay open till 8:00 or 9:00 p.m. Some convenience stores (often attached to gas stations) stay open until midnight. In large cities, corner delis and some supermarkets operate around the clock.

chapter five

TIME OUT

It is a cliché worth repeating: Americans work hard and play hard. They may exchange the trading floor for the gym or garden, but they approach their leisure time with the same energy and single-mindedness they apply to the workday. "Thank God it's Friday" means packing as much into the weekend as possible!

A snapshot of a typical suburban Saturday morning would reveal cars being washed, lawns mown, and home projects tackled. Media images may portray Americans as either sedentary couch potatoes or lycra-clad extreme athletes, but most fall comfortably in the middle. The great outdoors is America's playground. Even the workaholic will make time to play golf, hike, cycle, or ski. Excellent community facilities and subsidized programs mean that, compared to other countries, a wide range of recreational activities are accessible to most people. Closer to home, there are farmer's markets to visit, garage sales to browse, and get-togethers to organize.

For a nation of individualists, Americans are also "joiners." Eight out of ten belong to at least one club. This may be a civic group, such as the Rotary Club or Lions, a special interest organization, or a sports club. If Junior is playing Little League baseball, Dad (or Mom) is as likely to be coaching as sitting on the sidelines.

The constant quest for self-improvement has spawned an industry in educational seminars. Saturday mornings can be spent learning screenwriting or how to open a frozen yogurt franchise. Meanwhile, there's a cable channel or magazine for every interest, from Civil War buffs to orchid growers. Even more can be crammed in by multitasking— "taking baby for a walk" may mean pushing a jogging stroller for five miles while trying to beat a personal best! Sunday, for many, is reserved for church, and is the closest an American will come to a day of rest.

VACATIONS

Many Americans get just two weeks' annual vacation. This may be supplemented by long-weekend getaways, but it still means that even vacations are enjoyed at a frenetic pace. In contrast, school summer holidays have always been ten to twelve weeks long, the tradition originating in the need for children to help out on the family farm. Not many sixth graders have to pitch in with the harvest these days, so working parents are thankful for the range of local programs/activities and "sleepaway" camps to keep children busy.

SHOP TILL THEY DROP

As Gary Althen reminds us in *American Ways*, following the terrorist attacks of September 11 the country's leaders urged the reeling nation to resume their daily lives, implying, according to commentators, that they should go out and shop. New York Mayor Giuliani actually said, "Go shopping." Senator Tom Daschle said, "Buy that new car." The message was clear—in addition to shoring up the faltering economy, shopping would represent a comforting return to normalcy.

Even before the ideas of spending as a patriotic duty and retail therapy came into play, Americans have always loved to shop. How does one account for the staggering amount of consumerism in the United States? Is it the deserved fruits of one's labors, or economic one-upmanship in a classless society?

Less lofty explanations may simply be that because consumer goods are so cheap it makes more sense to replace that burned-out hairdryer than to get it fixed, leading to the perception of a disposable society. Transience in trends, reflecting the desire for constant change, means an American will buy today's look and replace it in a couple of years. Paradoxically, many Americans buy their clothes and housewares from the same high-street chains, perhaps indicating even individualism will be traded off for convenience in today's busy world.

Many items considered luxuries elsewhere are, in the States, considered essential to sustaining the way of life. That second car provides transport to work. TVs and computers in bedrooms mean family members have freedom of choice. A combination of high labor costs and the desire for privacy leads people to invest in labor-saving devices over household help. These in turn free up time and energy for more worthwhile pursuits. With an unwavering conviction that tomorrow will always be better, Americans know there will always be a way to pay. "Plastic meltdown" (credit-card debt) does not have the same stigma it has in other societies.

Through TV home-shopping channels and the Internet, spending can be a round-the-clock activity. For traditionalists who like to go to stores, shopping is easy. Keep the receipt to exchange goods or get a refund, no questions asked. Before you count out exact change, remember that in most states a sales tax (ranging from 2.9 percent in Colorado to 7.25 percent in California) will be added on to many items at the checkout. Sales are held on practically every holiday weekend at department stores.

The mall is the epicenter of suburban life. Here, families shop, eat, and go to the movies. Teens work part-time or simply gather and hang out. Grandma and her buddies may even power walk around the many safe, undercover miles it provides.

For the visitor, America is a shopper's paradise—both for the cheap prices and the fantastic range of goods. From high-quality Native American art to low kitsch Lady Liberty foam crowns, there's something for everyone.

SPORTS—PLAY BALL!
Sports in America is about seven-year-olds learning "team spirit" from the neighborhood Little League coach. It's also about big business. Top universities compete for sporting preeminence as well as scholastic achievement. Scouts are dispatched to watch promising high-school students, who may be offered college sports scholarships worth thousands of dollars. At the professional level, players' salaries reach into the stratosphere. The lines between sport and

business are further blurred as the competitive language of sport and business jargon become ever more interchangeable.

For a country that produces such outstanding players of individual sports, America does not fare well in truly global team events, such as World Cup soccer or rugby. The reason? There's simply no tradition for these sports and therefore little following. America prefers its homegrown sports, and all the nostalgia, rituals, and sideshow entertainment that accompany them. No real work is done at the office until the "Monday morning quarterback sessions" (postgame analyses) have taken place. At professional or college level, in stadiums or on TV, America's top three sports—basketball, football, and baseball— draw huge numbers. Americans may stray from their roots, but they always stay true to their hometown sports team.

The rules of each game are too complex to explain here. However, the sports-mad American will be only too happy to explain a game's intricacies at the ballpark or sports bar. It can be a great way to make friends—as long as you "root" for the right team!

Baseball
Baseball is affectionately referred to as "the national pastime." It has also been described as

the most democratic of sports, played by men of all heights and weights. The formfitting pinstripe uniform can't conceal the odd paunch, and tobacco is still chewed in the dugout, but don't try telling Americans that their "boys of summer" aren't athletes. They have the record-breaking stats to prove it!

Baseball evokes nostalgia like no other sport— just ask a Brooklynite of the childhood trauma of being told his beloved Dodgers were relocating to LA. For spectators, baseball is a participation sport, punctuated by traditions such as the "seventh inning stretch," the singing of "Take Me Out to the Ball Game," and the consumption of beer, pretzels, and "crackerjack." The April to October Major League season culminates in the World Series, a best-of-seven-games championship.

Basketball
Basketball started in 1891 when James Naismith, a minister, seeking a new game for boisterous YMCA youths, nailed a peach net on to a gymnasium wall. Today it is the only American sport to have been exported successfully around the world. Visitors will hear the sound of a bouncing basketball

everywhere in the States. Friends are made over "pick up" games on public courts; teens "shoot hoops" in suburban driveways, and dream of becoming the next Michael Jordan.

The National Basketball Association was formed in 1949. The season runs from September to April. Playoffs are held in May and the World Championship in June.

The National Collegiate Athletic Association (NCAA) features 270 teams and has a passionate following, rivaling that of the professional league. The college season climaxes with the "March Madness" tournament.

Football

American football was adapted from the English game of rugby. First played at the college level in the late 1800s, it was deemed so brutal that President Theodore Roosevelt insisted the game be made safer. Today, despite the full armor of helmets and padding, the game is as much about speed and strategy as strength.

The August-to-December National Football League season reaches fever pitch when the top two teams battle it out on "Superbowl Sunday" in late January. The championship final tops the TV ratings, as much for its humorous beer commercials and half-time extravaganza as for the game itself. The nation stops, friends gather, and sales in chips and dip skyrocket.

The highlights of the fall college football season are also the various "bowl games" played between the champions of the different college leagues, the "Rose Bowl" in Pasadena being the biggest.

Soccer
Soccer is popular as a participant sport,
 particularly among children, but has failed to fill stadiums at the professional level, despite the fact that America won the women's soccer World Cup in 1999.

HIGHLIGHTS OF THE SPORTING CALENDAR
National Ice Hockey League—season starts in October and culminates in the late May/early June Stanley Cup Championship
US Open Golf—mid-June
US Open Tennis—late August/early September
The Kentucky Derby (horse race)—first Saturday in May
NASCAR stock car racing—including the **Daytona 500** (February) and **Indianapolis 500** (May)

EATING OUT

Americans will find any excuse to eat out—to socialize, for instance, for convenience, or simply for the excellent value offered by those huge breakfasts, "early bird" specials, and all-you-can-eat-buffets.

It is difficult to think of an American national dish although comfort foods such as chicken pot pie, mac (macaroni) and cheese, and meatloaf probably come close. Many popular foods have been Americanized from the national cuisines of immigrants.

One can probably find the most authentic American food at the regional level, and the most intriguing names—bear claw, popover, jerky, or gumbo anyone? Southern cuisine is influenced by its French, African-American, and Mexican heritage. "Soul foods" include chicken-fried steak, biscuits and gravy, ham-hock stew, and collard greens. Louisiana is home to Creole and Cajun-style cooking. Local favorites are crawfish bisque, blackened catfish, and jambalaya (rice with ham, sausage, and shrimp). Mexican enchiladas, burritos, fajitas, and salsas have been enthusiastically embraced north of the border.

Midwestern European imports are evident in the Scandinavian fish boils, Polish pierogis, and

German bratwurst. In the Northeast the foods of different ethnic groups have become mainstream. At New York street fairs neighboring stalls sell Jewish knishes, Greek spinach pastries, and Italian ziti and cannoli. This region also offers the best of indigenous produce—maple syrup, turkey, corn, pumpkin—not to mention the world-class lobster and Baltimore crab cakes.

On the other side of the country, east meets west to create fusion cuisine—Pacific salmon served on a bed of Mexican salsa, or Montana beef tossed in a wok with Asian noodles and vegetables.

The Barbecue Wars

A "cookout" is simply an alternative name for a barbecue. A "cook-off," on the other hand, is an annual contest featuring chefs from Texas, South Carolina, and Kentucky, vying to assert their state's supremacy in the barbecue wars.

Dining Etiquette

There are few hard and fast rules of dining etiquette in this relaxed culture. When a group of friends dine out together, they usually "go Dutch," dividing the bill equally among the number of guests. Don't forget to add a 15 percent tip.

Americans generally cut their food with the knife in the right hand, and then switch the knife and fork. The knife is placed on the plate, and the food is eaten with the fork in the right hand.

A lot of food is eaten with the hands—fried chicken, French fries, and tacos, for instance—which is probably why napkins (serviettes) are used at even the most informal meals. Portions are huge, and at all but the most sophisticated restaurants it is acceptable to ask for a "doggie bag" for leftovers. These days no one even tries to pretend that the seafood risotto is really for Fido.

WHEN ORDERING

A la mode A scoop of ice cream added to pie.

PBJ A peanut butter and jelly sandwich. America's favorite!

BLT Bacon, lettuce, and tomato sandwich.

Hero A long (a foot or more), overstuffed bread roll. (Alt. **sub**, short for submarine)

Soda A generic term for any carbonated drink, such as Coke or 7-up!

Sunny-side up A regular fried egg.

Once over easy An egg that is fried on both sides.

FRIENDSHIP, AMERICAN STYLE

The Americans have to be the most open, fun,
friendly people on the planet, but their idea of
what constitutes a friendship may be different
from what you're used to, so you may need to
adjust your expectations accordingly.

Not for independent Americans is the sense of
duty and mutual obligation that characterizes
Asian relationships. They are far less likely to
impose on a friend to seek help in getting a job or
fixing their car. It seems people are always busy
and frequently moving on, so friendships are
often, by necessity, of a transitory nature. The
attitude is to seize the day and enjoy the
friendship while it lasts. If you run into a friend
again after losing touch, time is spent happily
catching up, not apologizing for the lack of
contact. The best friendships are considered to be
low maintenance and guilt free.

The warm smiles, the expressions of interest,
the generous gestures are all genuine. Those used
to Northern European reserve or the formal
ritualized courtship of Asia may think making
friends in the U.S.A. will be a breeze. Yet
newcomers can be confused and disappointed to
discover that a relationship may go no further
than surface friendliness. "Americans are friendly
to many," observes Australian psychologist and
former expatriate Charmaine Bourke, "but, like

most other cultures, admit relatively few to that 'inner circle' of deep friendship."

The good news is that this means you can feel free to accept—and extend—casual invitations. No plans for the weekend? You'll be readily invited to tag along to a ball game or party. You can relax and have fun without that nagging sense of indebtedness, or need to reciprocate, that weighs on other cultures.

Getting to Know You

Americans like to hit the ground running when it comes to getting to know someone. Their seemingly personal questions might seem intrusive to some cultures. For example, "Where did you go to school?" might trigger the defenses of a class-bound Englishman. Here, it is simply an attempt to speed up the getting-to-know-you process. This works in your favor. Feel free to ask questions or engage in a conversation on safe topics, such as sports, family, hobbies, pets. What will scare off an American? Perceived attempts to dominate their time or become overly dependent. It is important to read social cues, respect social boundaries, and not overstay your welcome.

So, now that you know what to expect, how do you go about meeting one of those 290 million Americans? As we have seen, Americans are doers, joiners, and organizers. According to the old joke, if you put two British people on a desert island, they'll form a committee. Two Americans are more likely to set up a raft-building club, or a professional association for survivors. They can't resist talking to someone who shares their particular passion, so whatever your professional or leisure interest, find a group and get involved.

A nation of networkers, Americans will generously extend introductions and make connections for you. Mention that you like to hike and someone will introduce you to their coworker's cousin's wife who knows all the best trails. They are also multitaskers who like to combine activities in order to feel productive. They will be happy to get to know you if you suggest taking in a basketball game, a museum exhibition, or a shopping expedition together. Bars and parties can be hit or miss in terms of meeting like-minded people, but if nothing else provide a fun night out.

After initial introductions, it may be assumed that you're doing okay or are happy to fend for yourself. Remember that Americans respect independence and privacy. If you do reach out, you will be met with generous offers of advice or help. If a commitment to friendship *is* made, Americans will sweep you off your feet with unparalleled enthusiasm and generosity.

Let's Do Lunch!

A recently arrived expatriate, Beth, was concerned. Everyone she met ended the conversation with "let's do lunch," but no one had called. Beth hadn't committed any terrible cultural *faux pas*. Like many visitors, she had misinterpreted the warm, open, American communication style for an indication of friendship. While her colleagues were demonstrating genuine interest and good intentions, the reality is that tight schedules may prevent people from following up. "We must get together" may not be an invitation but a polite way to bring closure to a conversation.

Come On Over

Once an invitation is forthcoming, relax and enjoy it. American hospitality is legendary. Dinner may be a formal, three-course affair on fine china, or a buffet on a paper plate. Informality rules and everyone pitches in. It is polite when invited to ask if you can bring something. Your offer may be politely declined, although close friends may be asked to bring a salad or dessert. At a "potluck dinner" everyone is assigned a dish to prepare to share the load. (Insider tip: offering to bring wine can be a preemptive strike if it's a struggle to make a five-bean salad.)

Holiday entertaining such as at Christmas or Thanksgiving is family style with guests serving themselves from platters of food that are handed around the table. Cocktail parties are popular to introduce a large number of people to each other—parents at the beginning of the school year, for instance, newcomers to the neighborhood, or as a get-together before a conference.

No one stands on ceremony. The greatest honor is not to be waited upon, but to be included and told "help yourself" and "make yourself at home." Offer to help out, but be prepared because you may be entrusted with barbecue duties! The enjoyment is in the pleasure of each other's company—not in the perfection of the meal or the service.

Protocol
These days there is little in the United States that truly offends, other than criticizing the country's institutions or way of life—never a good icebreaker in any culture. As a universal rule, it is also wise to steer clear of religion, money, and politics.

For a formal dinner, arrive within fifteen minutes of the indicated time; for a party, up to thirty minutes is fine (just don't arrive early). Unlike other social events, cocktail party invitations stipulate an end as well as a start time, which should be observed.

Dress code is usually smart casual unless a written invitation stipulates otherwise. For barbecues or picnics, take it down another notch and break out the shorts and sandals.

Greetings

The customary greeting is "Hi. How are you?" accompanied by a smile and an out-thrust hand. You are not expected to provide a detailed report on the state of your health. A similarly vague, upbeat "Fine. How are *you*?" is appropriate. When being introduced to other guests, first and last names are presented, which is an invitation to continue on a first-name basis. Titles are reserved for professional situations. Students used to call teachers, neighbors, and family friends by the last name—and even "Sir" and "Ma'am"—but this practice is being relaxed, although it may still be followed in parts of the "gracious South."

People are expected to mingle and introduce themselves to each other. Americans generally have polished social skills and exude self-confidence. If the prospect of walking into a room full of strangers triggers cold chills, there is, naturally, a self-help book: *How to Work a Room*.

Gifts

If invited for dinner, you can't go wrong with flowers, candy, or a bottle of wine (as long as your hosts imbibe). If you're a weekend houseguest, a "hostess gift"—a small decorative object, book, or CD—is appropriate.

CULTURE

For a long while, Americans imported their high culture from Europe. It wasn't until the nineteenth century that the country took its indigenous art forms seriously. Fusing the influences and experiences of its people, it has stamped its own, singularly American style on the world of art and culture. The U.S. is home to some of the world's best museums and galleries, but the visitor should also explore America's homegrown contributions to the creative arts.

America excels at making culture more democratic and less stuffy. While Americans still get decked out in their finery for the opera, casual dress is the norm at the theater. You'll see everything from cocktail dresses to shorts and sandals, evening purses to briefcases and backpacks.

Certainly, a subscription to the opera or symphony might be expensive, but you can always attend the many free outdoor events, or the affordable regional or experimental theater productions. There's something for every taste and budget. When it comes to tickets, local knowledge can save big bucks, so check with a friend or the hotel concierge to get the inside scoop on discounted tickets. The quintessential American experience? Sitting in a park listening to a free concert by the Boston Pops—a classical orchestra that plays popular all-American standards (with the obligatory backdrop of fireworks, of course.)

POP CULTURE

Today, pop culture is one of America's biggest exports, delighting eager consumers around the world. Some countries charge America with cultural imperialism, claiming the hearts, minds, and stomachs of their young people have been lost to *Friends*, Britney Spears, and McDonald's. The world's youth, like so many generations before them, are simply mesmerized by the images and possibilities that America offers.

Theater
American playwrights have tackled the country's social issues head on, entertaining and moving

generations of audiences. Notable authors include Arthur Miller, Eugene O'Neill, Tennessee Williams, Edward Albee, David Mamet, and August Wilson.

"Off Broadway"
The designations "off Broadway" and "off off Broadway" do not refer to proximity to the "Great White Way," but rather the size of the theater.

Opera and Symphony
Thanks to private philanthropy, most cities have their own symphony orchestra; several also boast an opera company. Perhaps the most evocatively American "classical" music is that of George Gershwin and Aaron Copland. Influenced by African-American rhythms and stories, Gershwin (1898–1937) is best known for his symphony *Rhapsody in Blue* and the opera *Porgy and Bess*. Copland (1900–90) captured the American landscape and spirit in his symphonies, opera, and film and ballet scores. What does patriotism sound like? A John Philip Sousa march. A marching band display or fireworks spectacular isn't complete without the "Stars and Stripes Forever."

Music

Perhaps the best way to experience America's
music is on a cross-country drive. Tune in to local
stations and you'll hear New York rap and hip
hop, Kentucky bluegrass guitar, Miami's Latin
rhythms, Nashville country, Louisiana zydeco, and
the sunny California surf sound. Live music can
be enjoyed at stops along the way—new bands in
college towns, swaying gospel-singing
church choirs, and rock 'n' roll giants at
major sports stadiums.

Early African-American blues and gospel from
America's cotton fields and churches evolved into
jazz and rhythm and blues (R&B). Jazz found its
voice in the street squares and funeral processions
of New Orleans and has undergone many
incarnations, including ragtime, swing, big band,
and bebop. The R&B sounds of James Brown and
Chuck Berry were popularized by Elvis Presley.
The music was further commercialized in the
1960s by the soul singers of Detroit's Motown
label and by the 1970s disco sound.

The equivalent of Britain's music hall, the
variety acts of America's vaudeville were developed
into the Broadway musical. The classic shows,
including *Showboat*, *Carousel*, and *Forty-Second
Street*, are regularly revived. Irving Berlin and Cole
Porter incorporated American themes, humor, and
pathos in their offerings—all sandwiched between

high-kicking, show-stopping numbers. Their
successors, Leonard Bernstein and Stephen
Sondheim for example, toned down the razzle-
dazzle, but retained the vitality, wit, and poignancy
in their treatment of contemporary themes.
Meanwhile, stick a pin in the American map and
you'll find a high-school production of *Grease*.

Books

America's literature explores the depth and
breadth of the country's experience. It spans the
groundbreaking horror stories of Edgar Allan Poe
and the idealism of the transcendentalist writers
Emerson and Thoreau, to the adrenaline-fueled
works of the "Lost Generation" writer Ernest
Hemingway and searing portrayals of the African-
American experience.

Film

A perfect melding of art, science, and big business,
America and the movies is a match made in
Hollywood heaven. American films have shaped
our sensibilities over the last eighty years, usurping
for many the role of literature in the process. A
modern-day expression of populism, film also
gives great insight into the American psyche.

In film, America has always paraded its sunny
idealism, its unwavering optimism, its belief in a
happy ending. It has also revealed its darker side:

the disillusionment of *Citizen Kane*'s American dream (1941), the post-Vietnam cynicism of *Coming Home* (1978), the absurdity of war in *Catch-22* (1970), the failings of its leaders in *All the President's Men* (1976).

Like a mirror that is held up to the changing face of American society, movies document and reflect back what the nation is thinking and feeling at a given point in time. Film has regularly taken the pulse of race relations in America, traced shifting historical perspective on the plight of the Native American, and captured the changing face of teenage angst from decade to decade.

Some lament that the Hollywood blockbuster has been "dumbed down," unfairly skewing the world's perception of American life. Whether the studios are dictating trends or simply giving the public what it wants, global  audiences just can't get enough. While multiplexes may be dominated by films of the action adventure, feel-good variety, most towns have an arts cinema, catering to the strong following for independent and foreign films.

TRAVELING

It can shock the visitor to learn that only 14 percent of Americans possess passports. But when faced with such a tempting array of destinations—from the imposing skylines of its major cities, to the jaw-dropping beauty of its national parks—the visitor begins to understand why few Americans stray from their own territory. The U.S.A. has a spectacular variety of landscapes, and offers every conceivable activity. Interested in history? Pick up a musket and participate in a Civil War reconstruction in historic Virginia. Need an adrenaline surge? Try backcountry skiing in Utah or white-water rafting on the swift Colorado. Want to escape? Lose yourself in the fantasy land of Disney World or Las Vegas. Simply put, there's enough variety to last a lifetime and the visitor is spoiled for choice!

This book is not designed to be an exhaustive travel guide; there is a plethora of wonderful travel books targeting different budgets and interests. However, for those who truly want to discover the people and places beyond the usual tourist traps, here are two pieces of advice. First, consider exploring one or two regions in depth, as opposed to darting from city to city. Secondly, eschew the motel and fast-food chains in favor of restaurants and B&Bs that offer local color and authenticity as opposed to corporate homogeneity.

GENERAL INFORMATION
Travel Documents
The U.S. Immigration and Naturalization Service rigorously scrutinizes all travel documents. Visitors are usually required to show a passport, U.S. visitor's visa, and  return plane ticket. A visa-waiver program applies to many European and other countries. Longer-stay travelers, such as students, will need a different type of entry visa and proof of finances.

Insurance
You can't predict every eventuality, so it is essential to take out comprehensive travel insurance for your trip. Coverage should include medical treatment, emergency repatriation, travel delays or cancellations, ticket loss, property theft or loss, and personal liability. Check to see if your credit card already covers car rental and/or travel insurance.

Health

The United States is relatively free of health risks but nevertheless visitors should take out the maximum possible health insurance. The multitiered U.S. healthcare system is complex and expensive. Unless it is truly an emergency, a visit to the ER (emergency room) should be avoided. A minimum walk-in fee (up to $300) will be universally applied. Hospitals will request a credit card or proof of insurance coverage before any diagnosis or treatment. If you do need to receive medical attention, rest assured that standards are extremely high. Any lingering pain once you return home is likely to be from hefty doctors' or hospital bills.

Emergencies

For police, fire, or ambulance services, call toll free 911.

$$$

In America, the challenge is not finding an acceptable form of payment, but hanging on to your money in this land of plenty! Travelers' checks are generally accepted in stores and hotels and are refundable if lost or stolen. ATMs are to be found on almost every street corner, and most accept foreign-issued bank cards. Credit cards are essential for making hotel and car rental reservations, Visa and Mastercard being the most widely accepted.

Security and Personal Safety

The terrorist attacks of September 11 have led to increased domestic security measures. Visitors should allow plenty of time for security checks at airports and public venues. Be sure to take photocopies of your passport, visa, and plane tickets and keep them separate from your travel documents.

In terms of personal safety, general commonsense rules apply. Beware of pickpockets in crowded areas. Avoid dark, deserted streets and empty train or subway cars. Use ATMs in daylight, preferably inside a bank. Use a "fanny pack" for carrying money. Leave passports and valuables in hotel safe deposit boxes. When renting a car, ask the agent to explain the safest route to your desired destination so as to avoid having to navigate a downtown area at night. Hitchhiking is not recommended. Most importantly, try to blend in and avoid looking like a camcorder-wielding, map-toting tourist.

In the wake of so many horrific stories of gun violence emanating from the United States, outsiders might question why gun ownership is not outlawed altogether. The "right to bear arms" (the Second Amendment) was enshrined in the

Constitution in the post-Revolutionary era to
equip local militias to defend their hard-won land.
Today the British pose less of a threat—and in
most of the 40 percent of American households
that have a gun, the firearms are legally registered
as being for personal protection or recreational
use. Gun ownership continues to be a matter that
polarizes American public opinion. Support for
the gun lobby tends to be regionally based, with a
heavy concentration in the hunting, shooting, and
fishing states. Visitors are advised that by steering
clear of both this emotional debate *and* unsafe
neighborhoods, they can avoid an encounter with
somebody exercising their Second Amendment
right!

Accommodation
The weary traveler has a huge range of
accommodation options catering to different
budgets and preferences. The choices range from
no-frills youth hostels to luxury resorts and New
Age spas, and everything in between.

Even campsites give an insight into the
broad spectrum of American
vacation habits, with dwellings
ranging from humble canvas tents
to motor homes on wheels for those
who like to take all modern
conveniences—including the

kitchen sink—on vacation. You can avoid soulless highway motels by hitting the back roads and enjoying the personal touch of moderately priced B&Bs and country inns.

Where's the Restroom?

Visitors are often surprised and dismayed at the scarcity of public lavatories in the U.S.A. Railway, bus, and service stations usually have them but better facilities are to be found in department stores, museums, and restaurants.

"Where Is It?"

The word "toilet" is considered vulgar. Use "bathroom" in a private house, "restroom" in a public facility, and "men's room" or "ladies' room" in a restaurant, theater, or hotel.

Flight Deals

For the savvy traveler, when it comes to domestic flights, it's a buyer's market. The existence of no-frills airlines and regular price wars among carriers make for a wide range of fare options (sometimes even for the same seat!). Securing the best deal means doing your homework, and possibly trading convenience for price. If you can be flexible, either book well in advance or pick up a last-minute discount price. If you're willing to fly during an off-peak season and to take a circuitous route involving change(s) of plane, you can further reduce travel costs.

HITTING THE ROAD
Driving

Ever since the first pioneers headed west in covered wagons, the United States has been a country on the move. Today, America still offers plenty of open roads, plus affordable car and gas prices. For the tourist, driving may offer freedom, but distances are so vast that a fly-drive package might be the best option. A driving deterrent for visitors to cities is the high price of parking garages, and the aggressive towing or clamping of cars that violate the sometimes complex street parking rules.

For those who still can't resist the romance of a road trip, they will find American drivers to be neither the most courteous nor the most aggressive (despite highly publicized reports of "road rage"). Americans will also tell you that they don't have to look at the license plate of the car in front to tell which state the driver is from. Apparently, there are great regional variations in styles of driving!

> ### SOME BASIC RULES OF THE ROAD
> - Be aware that driving laws vary slightly from state to state. Nevertheless, nationwide, you should wear seat belts, and never drive under the influence of alcohol or drugs.
> - Speed limits are strictly enforced by radar-toting highway patrol or sheriff's officers. Fines can be stiff. Speed limits range from 55 mph on urban roads to 65 or 75 mph on rural highways. In urban areas speed limits change frequently, particularly in the vicinity of a school, so watch for signs.

Driving Permits

While most car rental agencies will accept your national driver's license, an international license can be a valuable English-language photo ID document to carry with you. It must be issued in the same country as your driver's license.

Car Rentals

Car rental outlets exist everywhere, although rates will be more affordable outside the major cities and airports. Options range from opulent sedans or sporty convertibles to "rent-a-wrecks" for those with little pride and a budget to match. Remember to factor in the size of car, taxes, mandatory insurance, and gas mileage when comparison shopping to obtain the most favorable rates.

Bus

Movies often depict long-distance bus travel in the United States as a service for society's disenfranchised and misfits. The bus stations may seem a little seedy, but the truth is that bus travel offers a reliable service for the seasoned, low-budget traveler willing to sit for twenty-eight hours to get from New York to Miami.

Mass Transit

Perhaps because the U.S. is a car-dependent nation, public transport (or "mass transit") is generally not as comprehensive or efficient as in other countries. Exceptions are the subway systems of New York, Washington D.C., Chicago, and San Francisco, which service most tourist destinations, but are to be avoided at rush hour!

The standard of local bus services in towns and cities is highly variable. Buses do not have conductors and you may need to have exact change or a prepurchased token or ticket.

Big Yellow Taxi

Taxis generally run on a metered system and can be hailed on streets in some cities if the "for hire"

ROAD SENSE

- There are three types of major road. The letter "I" indicates an Interstate Highway, "U.S." a U.S. Highway, and "Rte" (route) a local or state highway.
- The system of interstate road numbers is as follows. Even-numbered interstates (for example, I-80) run east–west (with the lowest numbers starting in the west. Odd-numbered routes (I-15) run north–south (the lowest numbers starting in the south).
- An expressway is a high-speed divided highway for through traffic with fully or partially controlled access. Expressways have entrance and exit ramps, and may or may not have tolls. The term "expressway" can be used interchangeably with "thruway."
- A highway may or may not be divided, and typically goes through cities rather than bypassing them as expressways do.
- A turnpike is traditionally a toll road—although you may also have to pay tolls on thruways, expressways, and parkways. More important than trying to decipher the name and number designations is ensuring that you have a good map and small bills (notes) and coins for the toll collector!

sign is illuminated. One of the most publicized traits of cab drivers in large cities is their ethnic diversity, with a survey revealing that nine out of ten new drivers in New York are immigrants, hailing from eighty-four different countries. While this makes for interesting conversation, you should not assume that all drivers automatically know the way to your destination.

TRAINS

The names given to train routes (Twilight Shoreliner, California Zephyr, Sunset Limited, Empire Builder) conjure up a time when the rail system was the primary mode of transportation connecting the industrial Northeast to the new frontiers out west. Today, while the nationwide train system, Amtrak, is much maligned by Americans, train travel is still a relaxing way to cover a lot of ground.

Amtrak's intercity network is not as comprehensive as the bus routes, and can be as expensive as air travel. However, as most stations are in downtown areas, train travel can save the time and money spent getting to and from airports. Amtrak operates a shuttle service between its most popular destinations including

Boston, New York, and Washington, D.C., and for a premium fare offers the high-speed Acela trains.

FOOD AND DRINK OPTIONS

Visitors can be overwhelmed by the array of food options in America. In most towns everything is available from fast food to gourmet restaurants, and from regional specialties to all-American fare. If you are on the road, the major challenge will be to eat healthily and affordably. Avoid hotel coffee shops. Most diner menus offer homemade soups, salads, and fruit plates along with the inevitable fries and pancakes.

The decisions to be made when ordering can seem interminable. Do you prefer 1 percent or 2 percent fat milk in your coffee? Or perhaps soy milk, cream, or "half and half" (half milk, half cream.) Then there are the ten different ways of preparing eggs, an impossible variety of sandwich breads, and a bewildering selection of salad dressings to choose from. It may seem redundant to ask for "lite" maple syrup to accompany that towering stack of pancakes, yet people do.

Coffee Culture

The film *L.A. Story* offers a rare moment of Hollywood self-deprecation as everyone asks for customized cappuccino—a half decaf, half caff, skim soy mocha, hold the cinnamon. It is true that these days a cup of coffee can look more like an ice-cream sundae. Authentic Italian restaurants, particularly in the Northeast, have always served good coffee, but credit for sending the cappuccino global must go to a certain Seattle chain. Many use the chain's outlets as "virtual offices," holding meetings and interviews—even plugging in their laptops next to their latte.

Tea Drinkers Beware

If you order tea anywhere but in the most sophisticated establishments, you'll be unceremoniously served a cup of hot water with a teabag and a plastic stirrer—that is unless you're in the South, in which case you'll be asked if you want "sweet tea"—iced tea with sugar added!

"One for the Road"

American bars take many forms, yet they are not, as a rule, the social equivalents of the family friendly continental café or the British pub.

American ads may boast that water from the Rocky Mountains gives their beer its distinctive taste; visitors often claim they add a little too much of the stuff, making American beer weaker than its European counterparts. For beer connoisseurs, however, there are ample alternatives in the vast range of microbrewery and imported bottled beers. And, of course, the soils of California and Oregon produce world-class wines. Many bars feature a "happy hour" early in the evening, with heavily discounted drinks. It is customary to leave a small tip ($1) for the bartender on the bar.

Laws regulating the sale of liquor vary from state to state. In most states, the minimum drinking age is twenty-one and before entering an establishment where liquor is sold, patrons will be asked for a photo ID card (usually a driver's license) to prove their date of birth.

Smoky jazz bars are now a thing of the past. American smoking regulations are among the most restrictive in the world. Many states have reserved areas in restaurants or bars for smoking; others have banned it altogether.

BARTENDER!
Straight up—without water or ice
On the rocks—with ice
With a twist—with a piece of lemon
Salt or no salt around the rim—state your preference when ordering a margarita

TIPPING

Visitors should be aware that many workers in service industries receive the minimum wage and rely on tips to make a decent income. The expected amount varies but is more in tourist areas, larger cities, and better-class hotels, restaurants, or hair salons.

As a general rule, add 15 percent to a taxi fare. Hairdressers expect 10 to 15 percent. Allow $1 a bag for bellhops and airport porters (more if you're toting a trunk full of college books or an unwieldy ski bag).

A standard tip in a restaurant would be 15 percent—less if you sit at a diner's counter—and up to 20 percent in a good restaurant for excellent service.

As the state tax added to the bill is often in the region of 8 percent, many Americans simply double the tax to calculate the tip. This means that diners should estimate paying 25 percent above the actual price of the meal to include both tip and tax.

BATTEN DOWN THE HATCHES
Given the continent's extreme weather patterns, rarely a year goes by without one headline-

making natural disaster. These include hurricanes pounding the Gulf or the eastern seaboard, snowstorms paralyzing cities on the eastern seaboard, tornadoes tearing through "tornado alley" in the Midwest, and western forest fires, fueled by late summer winds and drought conditions. Fortunately, the U.S. meteorological services are able to predict conditions likely to produce extreme weather accurately, and residents in affected areas are usually well prepared to react to such occurrences. Nevertheless, seasonal weather patterns should be taken into account when planning your trip.

chapter **seven**

BUSINESS
BRIEFING

"Yankees and Dollars have such inextricable
association that the words ought to rhyme."
Ralph Waldo Emerson, Journal entry, 1840

The United States remains the wealthiest, most
productive country in the world, with a highly
diversified industrial and service-based economy.
However, it is rapidly losing the status of
sole economic superpower, as
globalization plunges it into a
complex, competitive environment.
One-third of American corporate
profits already comes from
international business.

American companies are responding
with their trademark vigor. To "stay ahead of the
curve" they are turning international competitors
into global partners, engaging in joint ventures
and forming strategic alliances. With a flurry of
free-trade negotiations, America is trying to secure
for domestic firms the same trade concessions

overseas that are granted to foreign companies in the U.S.A. On the domestic front, staying barely one step ahead of antimonopoly legislation, huge monoliths have been formed by a succession of mergers and buyouts.

The principal role of government in this market-oriented economy is as a consumer of private goods and services, although federal regulatory bodies have been busy recently ensuring corporate compliance and accountability in the wake of various scandals.

On the labor front, the strength and political influence of the trade union movement has diminished since its heyday in the 1930s, as former union strongholds, such as manufacturing, decline. Indeed, it is estimated that 60 percent of new jobs in the information-age economy require skills currently held by just 20 percent of the workforce. The growing skills, and resultant wealth, gap is likely to remain a long-term challenge for America's twenty-first-century politicians and employers.

As the lure of cheap labor drives production overseas, the "Made in the USA" label is becoming scarcer. All-American Levi jeans? Made in Bangladesh. Telephone technical support is more likely to be based in New Delhi than New York. Meanwhile, global consumers are ambivalent—they love American fast food but fear what has been dubbed "coca-colonization."

English remains the *lingua franca* of business, and American management philosophies are internationally embraced. Yet U.S. companies are learning that they can increase effectiveness—and be better global citizens—if they demonstrate cultural understanding and sensitivity overseas.

The economy has shown amazing resilience in the wake of the September 11 terrorist attacks and the accompanying economic downturn. America's work ethic, fueled by eternal optimism, continues to serve the country well.

SNAPSHOT OF THE AMERICAN WORKPLACE

The American working environment has changed drastically. With one eye on costs and the other on retention, employers are increasingly offering part-time or shared jobs, or outsourcing to external contractors. Change is constant as companies are restructured, work teams become "virtual," and flexible work arrangements become the norm.

Turnover is high because regular job-hopping is considered a necessary résumé builder. The cradle-to-grave job mentality is long gone. Employees are expected to take charge of their own career management. Employers expect ethical behavior and results; employees will give it their all—until a better job offer comes along.

Policies, procedures, and practices govern every aspect of company life. In addition to enforcing equal opportunity legislation, corporate America has introduced diversity initiatives, promoting the employment and advancement of women and minorities. Sensitivity training is given to prevent discrimination and sexual harassment.

Roles are flexible, hierarchy is fluid, and functions are specialized. In today's "flatter" organization there's no stigma attached to a lateral move to develop new skills, or even to reporting to a former "fast track" protégé. The organization is "boundaryless," which means that everyone is comfortable communicating up and down the pyramid, or across functional departments.

The length of the working day depends on the company, industry, and seniority of the employee. Administrative staff may do a straight nine to five, or put in "face time"—wanting to be seen at their desks. As we have seen, many workers, particularly professional people, may work excessively long hours, even sacrificing weekends and vacation days. Foreign visitors often notice a paradox—on the surface, workers are informal and socialize freely, yet the volume and pace of work seem intense, with everything stamped "urgent" and people always "busy."

A typical office has an open-plan layout with partitioned cubicles—although the boss still gets the corner office with the best view, four walls, and a door! Managers are expected to be accessible and keep an "open-door" policy. Schedules and privacy should be respected. All but the most senior executives answer their own phone and e-mail.

The office may briefly stop for a birthday or wedding or baby "shower" celebration during work hours, with coworkers all contributing to a communal gift. Commutes are long so there is little after-hours socializing. Companies usually arrange regular social events, however, such as a family picnic or softball game, or occasional Friday evening drinks.

Dress Code
Dress codes vary depending on the industry and corporate culture. Men typically wear dark suits, and women dresses or skirts or pant suits. Many companies have instituted "casual Fridays." For others, smart casual attire is permitted all week, unless a client meeting is scheduled. While this dress code allows for greater comfort, some grumble that it requires them to buy a second "uniform," usually chinos (khaki pants) with an open-necked shirt for men, and

casual skirt or pants and top for women. Professional clothes in general are expected to be of good quality but not overly stylish. Women's makeup and jewelry should be understated. If in doubt, always err on the side of conservatism. A confident posture, personal hygiene, and good grooming are all essential.

First Impressions

Remember, "you never get a second chance to make a first impression." You will be judged on your conduct and appearance. Sloppy manners or inappropriate behavior may sink a deal or relationship.

THE BOTTOM LINE

The Americans do not feel the need to know the people they do business with. Trust is placed in lawyers and contracts, not in people. Rules are made and applied universally to all. Deals are swayed by a client's reputation, by profit margins or delivery time—not by the nature of the relationship.

In this "high task," "low relationship" society everything is systematized. While Latin American employees may rely on the long-term patronage of a patriarchal boss to get ahead, newly appointed Americans are assigned a temporary "mentor" to help them navigate the new organization. Meanwhile, the savvy professional will develop a "network"—a loose-knit group of professional acquaintances who support each other on a reciprocal basis. Job-hunting is still a matter of who you know—80 percent of jobs are secured through networking contacts.

> ### SUCCESS FACTORS IN U.S. BUSINESS
> - Show energy and enthusiasm.
> - Take initiative and responsibility.
> - Behave with integrity and consideration for others.
> - Be positive, upbeat, assertive.
> - Deliver quality work within the deadline.
> - Be visible. Network!

MANAGEMENT STYLE

A good manager is expected to set goals, be action-oriented, and deliver results. The command-and-control style manager doesn't cut it here. To describe the preferred U.S. management style, the analogy of the sports coach is often used. The manager will provide strategy and resources, and then cheerlead from the sidelines as the player "runs with the ball." The approach is to empower a subordinate to show initiative, make decisions, and be an independent contributor. "Don't bring me a problem—bring me the solution" is the mantra. The plethora of management books suggests that while great leaders may be born, a good manager can be developed.

Managers are evaluated on developing others, as well as on their own performance. The annual appraisal is an inclusive process, with employees being evaluated against mutually agreed upon goals or objectives.

If You're Standing Still—You're Moving Backward

While older societies might rely on precedent for wisdom and direction, the Americans look to the future for their inspiration. They are masters of reinvention, of generating and managing change. They may seem impetuous to outsiders. According to Swiss interculturalist Thomas Zweifel (*Managing Global Teams*), Americans have a "just do it" approach to business. They prefer "learning by doing" to cautious planning. Business is a moving target, so problem-solving and decision-making will provide short-term solutions, and not be etched in stone.

WORKING AS A UNIT

The American workplace is increasingly a team-oriented environment. The definition of "team" here is a group of individuals who work together to achieve a common objective. As we noted when considering individualism, it is not the harmonious, consensus-driven model of Asia. Members are selected for their different areas of expertise, and may receive "team building skills" training to be a cohesive and effective unit.

The Team

Promoters of teamwork declare there's no "I" in team. Individualists wryly point out that the word does contain the letters "M" "E".

MEETINGS

Meetings can serve a variety of purposes, from an impromptu ten-minute team catch-up to a preplanned, lengthier affair, with a detailed agenda and recorded minutes. At the close, roles and tasks are assigned and an action plan with deadlines established.

As with many aspects of American life, a meeting is a democratic process. The seating plan is informal and an assigned facilitator rather than the most senior person may lead the proceedings. Individuals from all hierarchical levels are encouraged to contribute, and decisions are made by majority rule. Competing viewpoints are openly expressed, adding "creative tension" to the process. For the most part, individuals diplomatically acknowledge each other's point of view and "piggyback" (build) on each other's ideas.

Newcomers are often shocked to note how everyone competes for the floor, sometimes with seemingly redundant statements. Stemming from the educational system, individuals are evaluated on the level of their participation as well as the quality of contributions. Social Darwinism prevails even in meetings, and you need to take every opportunity to make your mark, so speak up. Although brainstorming meetings may be a little too unstructured or wacky for some people, the Americans find them an effective way to generate creative ideas or solutions.

For a successful meeting, be punctual (phone if you're running late), be well presented, and be meticulously prepared.

NEGOTIATIONS
The American negotiating style tends to be a "hard sell"—sometimes characterized as sledgehammer

subtlety combined with missionary zeal! A strong
pitch about a product's, or individual's, strengths
may sound boastful but is meant to inspire
confidence and trust. It is also consistent with the
penchant for logical reasoning, directness, and
comfort with self-promotion.

American negotiators may have little
familiarity with, or patience for, the formal
business protocol, indirect communication style,
or consensual decision-making practices of other
countries (a fact that savvy international
negotiators often use to their advantage!). Their
focus is on the short term and the "big picture":
securing the best deal in a timely manner. Their
approach is informal, cordial, and
straightforward. The U.S. team will reveal its
position and expect the other party to engage in a
competitive bargaining process. If an impasse is
reached, American tenacity, creativity, and
persuasiveness will come to the fore. Despite the
"hard sell" tactics, negotiating partners should not
feel pressured into making a decision. The
Americans expect their counterparts across the
table to be similarly pragmatic and single-minded
in trying to secure a favorable deal. The greatest
source of frustration for American negotiators is
feeling that they are being "strung along," or that
their negotiating partners don't have the authority
to make the necessary decisions.

Note: Americans like to walk away from a meeting having secured a verbal agreement: the details will be hammered out later. Thus, a handshake may "seal the deal," but the agreement isn't in place until the ink on the contract is dry!

Case Study

The Tokyo-based negotiations between an American company and a Japanese vendor, having started well, unraveled on the last day. The Americans were focused on "bottom line" details: price and delivery dates. The Japanese were more concerned about process—and trust. Whenever the Japanese paused to reflect carefully on their counterparts' position, the Americans jumped in to fill the pause. The Americans interpreted the Japanese silence around the table as intransigence; the Japanese construed the American discomfort with silence as an unwillingness to listen. Clearly each party had come to the table equipped with their negotiating strategy, but with little understanding of the other party's cultural style.

PRESENTATIONS

Style or substance? When making a presentation, the Americans will expect you to have both. Some cultures are more literal in approach, others prefer lengthy discussions to build trust. By contrast, the Americans are visually oriented and prefer their presentations to be entertaining and high tech. A brisk pace, persuasive tone, and anecdotal evidence are used to outline a proposal's merits. As the MTV generation rises in the corporation, attention spans get shorter. Typical sessions will be brief (thirty to forty-five minutes) and well structured. Written handouts, including hard data and copies of the presentation slides, are usually distributed. Time for feedback or a "Q & A" (question-and-answer session) will be allocated.

A "CAN DO" ATTITUDE

In one of America's best loved children's books, "The Little Engine That Could" huffed and puffed her way up a steep hill. As she progressed her confidence increased, her mantra changing from "I think I can" to "I know I can." This "achievement orientation" may appear arrogant to outsiders, but is a cherished ideal and a powerful inner motivator that propels Americans forward in their pursuit of excellence.

Perceptions of behavior depend on the particular cultural lens you're looking through. To the visitor, American hyperbole may seem like exaggeration, that confident walk like an arrogant swagger. An American will tell you that they are taught to believe in themselves, put their best foot forward, and stand out from the crowd. In such a big country, survival of the fittest rules. As one mid-level manager put it, "To compete, I need to be both my own best product *and* sales promoter." Professional people even hone their "elevator pitch," encapsulating in thirty seconds who they are and what they do.

WINNER TAKES ALL

A visitor watching U.S. Olympic coverage was shocked to witness the TV commentator ask the "gold medal shoo-in," who took silver, "So what went wrong?" In this culture, as famed football coach Vince Lombardi said, "Second place is the first loser."

Competition can be seen in every walk of life from beauty pageants to "employee of the month" to July 4 hot-dog-eating contests. The drive to be first, highest, quickest, or just plain best has inspired Americans to accomplish extraordinary feats—but you'll only know the names of those who came first as "winner takes all."

WOMEN IN BUSINESS

Women represent almost half of the workforce. They are well represented at the management level and are increasingly making their mark in nontraditional fields. However, many contend that subtle discrimination still exists, preventing women from rising above the "glass ceiling" and penetrating the upper echelons of organizations. In terms of advancement opportunities, many working mothers feel they are diverted from the "fast track" to the "mommy track." Flexible hours, child care, and pay parity remain hurdles.

Women expect to be treated the same as men although still appreciate displays of etiquette. For men, this means your female counterpart is just as likely to pick up the restaurant bill but may expect *you* to pour the coffee.

BUSINESS ENTERTAINING

Foreign business visitors should not expect VIP treatment. Even the most senior executive will not be picked up from an airport or hotel. Business entertaining is only likely to occur for a specific reason: to impress a potential client or for a "deal-closing" dinner. Don't let the informal dress and social chit-chat fool you. Americans take their business seriously. Behavior is relaxed but relatively restrained. The two-martini lunch has become the two-Perrier lunch. If in doubt about ordering an alcoholic drink, even at dinner, take your cues from your host. The meal will start with small talk but quickly get down to business. Cocktail parties are juggling acts—make sure you always have one hand free of food and drink to greet people!

Finally, there are strict policies discouraging the receiving and giving of gifts in the corporate world to avoid appearances of impropriety.

chapter eight

COMMUNICATING

LINGUISTIC TRADITIONS

From street slang to psychobabble, business jargon to catchphrases, the American language provides a window into the ever-changing culture. The Americans have always loved to share their thoughts and feelings. Benjamin Franklin's homespun proverbs and Mark Twain's witticisms have been handed down through the generations from the rocking chair. In the new millennium, philosophy is laced with humor and more likely to come from a fridge magnet, bumper sticker, or any book with "Zen" in the title. If a person doesn't get the joke, they're "not the sharpest tool in the shed."

Historically, language has been at the forefront of defining America's distinct cultural identity. Connecticut's Noah Webster published the first American-English dictionary in 1806, believing that the development of a distinctive American language was a further mark of independence from the British. Webster's dictionary included new American vocabulary, such as skunk and chowder. Webster also modified needlessly complicated spellings, changing centre to center, plough to plow, and colour to color.

More recently, Americans have debated whether immigrant children should be provided with bilingual education. While the wheels of government turn slowly on such issues, corporate America acts. TV and radio stations targeting different language groups abound. The language of billboards reflects the demographics of the neighborhood. Phone companies offer menu selections in Spanish; bank ATMs add Chinese to the options.

Currently, it is estimated that one in five people speak a mother tongue other than English at home. With 40 million speakers, Spanish is the second-most spoken language in the U.S.A. Meanwhile, there are still enclaves that operate exclusively in the language of the old country—Yiddish is common in certain parts of Brooklyn, and the Amish communities of Pennsylvania and Ohio communicate in a dialect of German.

In her *USA Phrasebook*, Colleen Foster lists some of the words borrowed from other languages that have been incorporated into the American lexicon. These include nitty-gritty (African), moose (Native American), chocolate

(Aztec), tycoon (Chinese), saloon (French), chutzpah (Yiddish), and glitch (German). The all-American hamburger? Also German.

Divided by a Common Language

George Bernard Shaw is reputed to have said that America and England were "two countries divided by a common language." There are differences in spelling, vocabulary, and idiom. To table a motion means to put something on the agenda in the U.K.; in the U.S. it means to remove it. The British stand for election while dynamic Americans run for office. Americans break the ice; milder mannered Brits melt it.

COMMUNICATION STYLE

Have a great day! Terrific suit! Nice job! American exchanges generally tend to be informal, laced with superlatives, with an exclamation point on the end. Everything is given a positive twist, a "challenge" euphemistically being transformed into an "opportunity."

In most situations, Americans pride themselves on treating everyone in the same upbeat, friendly manner. They will expect to be on first-name terms, regardless of age or rank. Occupational titles such as Doctor, Officer, or Professor may be used at work only. The title "Ms." covers both married and unmarried women, but is mainly used in written communication. Names are often shortened and nicknames are common.

Americans excel at remembering—and making frequent use of—the first names of the people they meet.

Generally with Americans, what you see (or hear) is what you get, particularly in business. There's no "beating around the bush." "Honesty is the best policy" so directness is preferred over politeness and diplomacy. This may sound blunt to the European ear, used to an eloquent discourse or intellectual debate. Americans, however, prefer exchanges to be brief, clear, and precise—preferably delivered in a sound bite.

Quick off the Mark
Picture this: a German completes a business presentation to three clients. The Japanese sits back and respectfully considers what he's heard. The English woman mentally formulates a carefully constructed, articulate response. The American? Jumps right in. Timing and spontaneity are of the essence. It's important to show you can think on your feet, "tell it like it is," and act quickly. It all comes down to performance and results.

The style of thinking is a linear progression through a logical sequence of facts to one clear conclusion—cause and effect, connect the dots. Americans place trust in objective, concrete facts and data. Information is conveyed in the explicit verbal message. There is no need for subtle, nonverbal gestures, hidden meanings, or extraneous information. Just the facts, ma'am, will do. Written reports will be headed with a brief "executive summary"—probably written in bullet points.

Everyone seems to be available 24/7 (twenty-four hours a day, seven days a week) and to expect a quick response. Voice mail is used extensively—people sometimes intentionally call when someone's out so they can leave a quick message. Tag! It's now *your* turn to respond. In the same vein, colleagues in adjoining cubicles will sometimes e-mail each other—it's fast, it's efficient, and a "paper trail" is left. All phone and e-mail communications should be brief and to the point.

The Paper Trail

From the penning of the Constitution to today's litigious business environment, Americans trust only what's written down. In such a large and diverse country, one can't assume that everyone's "on the same page" (in agreement) and people must "cover their tracks" (document everything), so "get it in writing."

Managing Disagreement

The Americans express their ideas and emotions freely, although profanity is frowned upon. Table thumping and temper outbursts may indicate poor self-control but are tolerated as "pressure under fire." Personal disputes are considered disruptive and are handled with customary American pragmatism. "Conflict resolution" is widely used in corporations and the lower echelons of the legal system. A facilitated, structured process, it allows parties to reach resolution by expressing their respective feelings and needs.

CARRY A CARD!

Everyone carries business cards, and these are casually exchanged during introductions. They won't be respectfully scrutinized, Asian style, and indeed may be tucked directly into a wallet.

Your card should bear your name, company, title, and job function, along with your phone and fax numbers, e-mail address, and office address.

Sporting Talk

The competitive world of sports provides perfect analogies for American business speak. American managers dutifully espouse the latest buzz words—boundaryless, value-added, reengineering paradigms—but are more comfortable "stepping up to the plate" to "hit a home run"! Approximate figures are described as "in the ballpark."

In their enthusiasm, they can forget that even fellow English speakers may not share the same sporting terms of reference (in which case their Aussie and English counterparts may slyly remind them by informing them they're on a "sticky wicket"!).

Small Talk

"So, how about those Mets?" "Hot enough for ya?" A casual conversation is often opened with a rhetorical question. Small talk is confined to safe topics—TV programs, sports, the weather. The usual suspects (sex, money, religion, and politics) are taboo. Small talk will abruptly end when it's time to "get down to business."

Silence isn't Golden

What makes an American feel uncomfortable? Silence! If there's a lull in the conversation, they feel compelled to jump in and fill it. One person picks up where the other left off— to interrupt or talk over someone is considered rude. At the opposite extreme, being overly longwinded isn't appreciated, either. Congressional speakers, Oscar winners, and meeting participants alike are often given just thirty seconds to make their point before being unceremoniously cut off.

Manners

Manners are relaxed and informal but very much in evidence. "Please" is commonly used. "Yes please" in response to being offered something might be replaced by "sure" or "okay," which may sound a little brusque to some ears. "Thank you" or "thanks" might be answered with a chipper "sure," "no problem," or slightly more formal "you're welcome." "Excuse me?" is the equivalent of the British "What did you say?" "Pardon?" or "Sorry?" And every stranger within earshot will "bless you" after you sneeze! Finally, with no door to knock on, "the jury's still out" on appropriate protocol for approaching a colleague's cubicle in an open-plan office.

Political Correctness

This is one area where America is not quite so relaxed. Society and the workplace have to some extent been "sanitized" to ensure that no one is offended and everyone is included. Such gender-neutral terms as chairperson, firefighter, and mail carrier are commonplace. African-Americans and Native Americans are finally being addressed on their own terms. The result is an office communications culture that is relatively guarded. Visitors often note that Americans don't seem to "let their hair down" even at the office party. Remember, in the workplace, personal comments (even compliments) directed at a member of the opposite sex should be avoided, lest they be misconstrued as inappropriate or unwelcome— grounds for a sexual harassment charge.

BODY LANGUAGE

Handshakes are firm and accompanied by a smile and direct eye contact. This establishes credibility, conveying confidence and sincerity. In terms of a conversational "comfort zone," Americans prefer to keep at an arm's length distance, although they may touch another's arm as a gesture of warmth or to emphasize a point.

In some cultures the degree of formality increases as one climbs the hierarchy. Not so in the U.S.A. where there is less "power-distance" between ranks. How do you detect "who's the boss" in a meeting? Not by seating arrangements or displays of deference, but by the relaxed yet authoritative style.

In terms of nonverbal gestures, it is difficult to generalize across regions without lapsing into stereotypes, but here goes. The Texans are renowned for their backslapping bonhomie, Midwesterners are more self-contained, Italian Americans gesticulate with their arms more than German Americans. High-fiving is commonplace among close friends, although a little gauche for the baby-boom generation.

Nonverbal gestures are always a cross-cultural minefield. For example, to indicate "good," an American might form thumb and forefinger into an "o" shape, a gesture that could be considered offensive elsewhere. Better to stick to the universal thumbs up to express approval.

HUMOR

The *Asian Times* journalist known as Spengler observed that there is an absence of characteristically American jokes as there are no all-American characteristics. True or not, Americans will readily admit that they reserve the sharpest put-downs for their neighboring state!

Other than the obligatory icebreaker at the beginning of a presentation, Americans may appear to take themselves a tad more seriously than exuberant Brazilians or irreverent Australians. This may be because their sense of humor is different. It is also used more circumspectly. Again, the style of humor varies according to regional preferences and imported ethnic influences. American humor can range from the cool, acerbic, cosmopolitan wit of *Frasier* to the gentle, wry, nuanced storytelling of the heartland's Garrison Keillor. As with so many aspects of American life, Jewish people have made an inordinate contribution to the world of comedy and entertainment. The observational humor and ironic twists of today's iconic Jewish comedians, such as Woody Allen and Jerry Seinfeld, have an international appeal.

The preferred style may vary but Americans like to surround themselves with humor. It is considered a national birthright to have a good time. In what she describes as the nation's "pursuit of fun," Dr. Eun Kim (*The Yin and Yang of American Culture*) observes "most Americans must have a good dose of humor on a daily basis." Americans get their fun fix from TV sitcoms and comedy clubs, best-selling books, and e-mail jokes.

The American home and office is festooned with cartoons on bulletin boards, and joke-a-day calendars. Just remember, you're in the land of PC, so avoid telling off-color jokes.

THE MEDIA
Television

Not for the Americans the bleak lives portrayed in Britain's soaps, or the intense character studies of European movies. They prefer to remove themselves from the daily grind and escape to a fantasy world where everyone is glamorous and the good guy always wins.

There are three network TV stations but cable and satellite options boost the number of available channels into the hundreds. Americans can watch round-the-clock news, sports, and sitcom reruns. In fact, many apparently do. An average of seven-and-half hours of TV is watched daily in the average American home. Special interest channels cater to more esoteric tastes. Reality TV still rules the airwaves as Americans seem transfixed by watching people eat bugs or paint dry on makeover shows. For the more discerning viewer, there is the Public Broadcast System. Funded by viewer donations and corporate sponsorship, it offers news analysis, educational programming, and British imports.

Gone are the days when TV's married couples slept in separate beds. The viewing public now countenances gay characters and single parents on prime time. However, the Puritans have cast a long shadow. Expect to see far less sex—but far more violence—on America's TV screens than on European ones.

News

With a total of 10,544 FM and AM radio stations, 1,663 TV stations, and 1,573 daily newspapers, the U.S.A. is tuned in, turned on, and up to speed.

While *U.S.A. Today* is a national paper, most of America's newspapers cater to a specific town or city. Quality newspapers include the *New York Times*, *Washington Post*, *Boston Globe*, and *Los Angeles Times*. Additionally, there are weekly news magazines (*Time*, *Newsweek*, etc.) for real news junkies. Despite this, 69 percent of people get their news from TV or the Internet, with 63 percent ranking TV as the most believable news source.

POSTAL AND ELECTRONIC COMMUNICATION

The postal service is reasonably reliable and inexpensive. Post offices open from 9:00 a.m. to 5:00 p.m. To avoid a lengthy wait, go at off-peak hours. Stamps can also be bought at some supermarkets and even online. The post office does not offer the wide range of goods (such as stationery items) or services (such as bill paying) offered in many countries.

Mail for travelers can be sent to any U.S. post office. It must be marked "General Delivery" and include the post office zip (postal) code. To pick up a package, you will need to show a picture ID.

Go to www.usps.com on the Web for information on rates, zip codes, etc.

Private carriers such as FEDEX or United Parcel Service (UPS) are expensive, but their home pick-up service makes them a fast and convenient option.

Telephones
Public phones are plentiful but are increasingly being converted to credit- or phone-card use only. Since deregulation, rates have become so competitive among the numerous phone companies that many households have two different carriers for the same line, one for local and one for long distance.

Most people have an answering machine or voice-mail service and also "call waiting" so calls aren't missed and can be answered when convenient. Mobile phones, many with text-messaging services, ensure that people can be available 24/7.

While phone rates in the U.S.A. are comparatively inexpensive, hotel phone rates are exorbitant. Calls can be made collect, by credit card, or with a prepaid calling card.

Your home mobile phone may not work in the U.S.A. because of the difference in frequencies. Even if it does, it will be expensive. You might consider renting a local cell phone with prepaid minutes.

If you are calling the U.S.A. from overseas, dial your country's international access code (e.g., 00 from the U.K.), the U.S. country code (1), the three-digit area code (e.g., 212 for New York), then the seven-digit phone number. Thus for New York 123 4567, you would dial, from the U.K., 001 212 123 4567.

USEFUL NUMBERS

Information (Directory Assistance): 411

Emergencies: 911

Operator: 0

International Operator: 00

Internet Cafés

Libraries, airports, hotel business centers, and of course Internet cafés, all allow you to get online. For laptop devotees, you'll need an AC adapter and a plug adapter.

Faxes
While the advent of the Internet is gradually making the fax obsolete, fax services are still offered at most hotels, newsdealers, and copy shops.

CONCLUSION

In a 2000 survey, Americans expressed their concern over the state of democracy, the failings of equal opportunity, and declining moral standards. However, an astounding 72 percent of American respondents still declared themselves proud of their country, compared to 49 percent of British and 39 percent of Italians. This is testimony to the fact that, while its founding principles face challenges in these increasingly complex times, it is the continued pursuit of these ideals—the upward march to the "city on a hill"—that sets America apart.

CultureSmart! USA has set out a framework to enable you to appreciate this rich and fascinating country at many different levels—the individualism, the distinct regional characters, and the overarching "Americanness" of it all! An understanding of the many cultures that make up America, and of the attitudes and behaviors you are likely to meet, will help you in business and in pleasure—and make you a better guest. Your visit will be all the more rewarding for it.

Now that you have a sense of what to expect, it is time to plan your visit. Where to start? How do you put your arms around a giant? Quite simply, you don't. You take it one state, one town, one main street, one serendipitous encounter at a time. By all means head for the iconic landmarks, the Grand Canyon, Niagara Falls, the Empire State Building, or the Alamo. But remember always that the most memorable and enriching experiences to be had in this great land are in the encounters with the people along the way.

Further Reading

Althen, Gary, with Amanda R. Doran and Susan J. Szmania. *American Ways: A Guide For Foreigners in the United States*. Yarmouth, Maine: Intercultural Press/London: Nicholas Brealey Publishing, 1988, 2003.

Bryson, Bill. *Made in America*. Great Britain: Martin Secker & Warburg Ltd., 1994.

Carruth, Gorton, and Eugene Ehrlich. *American Quotations*. New York: Gramercy Books, 1988.

Copeland, Anne P., and Georgia Bennett. *Understanding American Schools: The Answers to Newcomers' Most Frequently Asked Questions*. Boston: The Interchange Institute, 2001.

Cotter, Colleen (coordinating author). *U.S.A. Phrasebook: Understanding Americans and their Culture*. Melbourne/Oakland/London/Paris: Lonely Planet Publications, 1995, 2001.

Hall, Edward T. *Beyond Culture*. New York: Anchor/Doubleday, 1976.

Kennedy, Caroline. *A Patriot's Handbook*. New York: Hyperion, 2003.

Kim, Eun Y. *The Yin and Yang of American Culture: A Paradox*. Yarmouth, Maine: Intercultural Press/London: Nicholas Brealey Publishing, 2001.

Lanier, Alison R., revised by William G. Gay. *Living in the U.S.A.* Yarmouth, Maine: Intercultural Press/London: Nicholas Brealey Publishing, 1973, most recent edition 1996.

Lipset, Seymour Martin. *American Exceptionalism: A Double-Edged Sword*. New York: W. W. Norton & Company, Inc., 1996.

Lyons, James, et al. *Lonely Planet USA*. Melbourne/Oakland/London/Paris: Lonely Planet Publications, 1999, 2002.

Stewart, Edward C., and Milton J. Bennett. *American Cultural Patterns: A Cross-Cultural Perspective*. Yarmouth, Maine: Intercultural Press and London: Nicholas Brealey Publishing, 1972, 1991.

Walmsley, Jane. *Brit-Think Ameri-Think: A Transatlantic Survival Guide*. First published in Great Britain by Harrap Ltd., 1986. Published by the Penguin Group, New York/London/Melbourne/Ontario/Auckland, 2003.

Wanning, Esther. *Culture Shock! USA*. Portland, Oregon: Graphic Arts Center Publishing Company/London: Kuperard, 1991.

Zweifel, Thomas D. *Culture Clash: Managing the High-Performance Team*. New York: SelectBooks, Inc., 2003.

Index

Acknowledgments

With thanks to Jack and Caroline for their patience, and Sonja Schlegel-Breemen, Cathe Tansey, and Jo Parfitt for their inspiration. Special thanks to Alan Beechey, cultural observer and writer extraordinaire.